Undiluted

Rediscovering the Radical Message of Jesus

Benjamin L. Corey

DESTINY IMAGE® PUBLISHERS, INC.

P.O. Box 310, Shippensburg, PA 17257-0310

"Promoting Inspired Lives."

This book and all other Destiny Image, Revival Press, MercyPlace, Fresh Bread, Destiny Image Fiction, and Treasure House books are available at Christian bookstores and distributors worldwide.

For a U.S. bookstore nearest you, call 1-800-722-6774.

For more information on foreign distributors, call 717-532-3040.

Reach us on the Internet: www.destinyimage.com.

ISBN 13 TP: 978-0-7684-8890-6

ISBN 13 Ebook: 978-0-7684-8906-4

For Worldwide Distribution, Printed in the U.S.A.

2 3 4 5 6 7 8 / 18 17 16 15 14

Dedication

For Adonis Vidu, who taught me that God's story
is way bigger than I ever imagined,

and

For Dean Borgman, who taught me that I had
a very important part in the story.

Acknowledgments

This book only exists because the journey occurred, which means that first and foremost, I wish to thank my wife, Tracy. Thank you for believing that God had more for my life, for believing we could find a Christianity worth living, and for not giving up in pushing me toward seminary. The person I am today is only because of your influence—without you, I wouldn't have discovered any of this. I will forever be thankful that you were part of this journey of faith.

I wish to thank all of the faculty and staff at Gordon-Conwell and Fuller Theological Seminary who have played a part in my faith journey. Most especially Dr. Adonis Vidu: thank you for your kindness, generosity, and inspiration. Dean Borgman, while you probably don't even remember who I am, you ruined my life—thank you! Dr. Paul Martindale, thank you for teaching me how to separate culture from my faith—that was perhaps one of the most useful things I learned in seminary. Dr. David W. Gill, thank you for helping me to rediscover the radical, countercultural life that can be found in the beatitudes.

To all of my friends back in the North Shore, thank you. Phil Wyman, you have always inspired me with your undiluted love for people. Jeff Gentry, thank you for authenticity and for inviting me into a new world. To everyone in the Chang's life group and all the folks who were part of Vida Real, thank you for teaching me about community and doing life together. A special thanks to Chris and Melissa, and Sarah and Karlos for being available on a moment's notice during the rough chapters.

To those who continue to shape my present journey, thank you for the many ways in which you walk beside me. Dr. Joe McGarry—a mentor, friend, and the older brother I never had—you have continually been a source of encouragement during this journey. Rogier van Bakel, my favorite ("friendly") atheist in the whole world, thank you for your friendship over the years. To the many MennoNerds out there—thank you for showing me that I hadn't really discovered anything new at all, but simply rediscovered what the Anabaptists have known about God all along. Brian McLaren, thank you for your kindness and shaping my journey in more ways than you know. And, to my friend Frank Schaeffer, thank you for opening doors for me when I was too short to open them on my own—I will always be grateful.

Perhaps most importantly, to my daughter, Johanna: everything I need to know about God, I learned from adopting you. I pray that your roots will grow deep in God's love so that you will experientially know how wide, how long, how high, and how deep is his love for you.

And, of course, to the folks at Destiny Image—thank you for believing that this is a story that needed to be told.

"Follow me."

—JESUS OF NAZARETH

Contents

The Backstory

Some people say that going to seminary could cause one to lose his or her faith. In my case, I supposed you could say that's true.

In the fall of 2008 I arrived at Gordon-Conwell Theological Seminary in South Hamilton, Massachusetts, with a potent mix of arrogance and brokenness. Even though I had never as much as set foot on the grounds of a theological institution of the caliber of Gordon-Conwell, I arrived at the doorstep thinking that I had very little to learn about God and the ways of Jesus.

This is a memoir about how wrong I was. It's also a story about how wrong we often are.

As Christians in America, we're often lulled into the false belief that somehow we have a monopoly on the pure and undiluted version of the message of Jesus. Unfortunately, we don't. Christianity by nature has a tendency to blend in and become obscured by the cultural influences that surround it—such has been the case for nearly 2,000 years of Christian history.

Our experience is no different.

The forces of culture around us, whether American culture or even Christian culture, slowly creep into our faith over time. Before we know it, we're living out a diluted version of the Christian faith—a hybrid of Jesus and America, while mistakenly believing that somehow we're the only ones who are following the pure and undiluted version of the message of Jesus.

Well, we're not.

The version of Jesus that so many of us live out is something that fits snugly in our lives, existing in near-complete harmony with the culture around us. However, the radical message of Jesus was never intended to fit neatly into any culture—it was countercultural from the very beginning, and remains so today.

We all, in some ways, are living out a watered-down, diluted version of the radical, countercultural message of Jesus. As a result, many of us have grown discontent with the faith that has been passed down to us and have realized we are trapped in a religion that seems to offer us far less than what we imagined Jesus could be.

We want more.

Not in a greedy American way, but in a "we won't accept any cheap substitutions" kind of way.

This book is in part the story of how I embraced death to the Christian religion I arrived at seminary with, and how I exchanged it for a vibrant life following the radical message of Jesus.

It's also a book about how you can rediscover the radical message of Jesus—especially the parts that are often watered-down or completely left off by American Christianity.

In doing so, you might experience a few deaths.

Death to old ideas.

Death to old beliefs.

Death to old understandings.

However, the way of Jesus has always been a radical invitation to experience death that gives birth to new life.

There's new life to be found in rediscovering the radical message of Jesus.

New life to be found in casting aside our nets.

New life to be found in picking up a cross…

There's new life to be found in the radical message of Jesus.

Now, just to be clear: this isn't a book that claims I have once and for all discovered a pure form of following Jesus. Nor is this book an academic work that claims to adequately cover all of the subjects it brings up. This book is none of those things.

Instead, this is a book about my journey.

It's a book about change.

It's a book about rediscovery.

It's a book about my journey of change and rediscovery that led me to embrace a Jesus who was a little more...

A little more countercultural,

A little more radical,

And a little more...

Undiluted.

CHAPTER 1

Undiluted

But whoever drinks the water I give them will never thirst (JOHN 4:14).

The other night I was cooking some rice for dinner and quickly realized I had made a crucial mistake: I measured the water-to-rice ration incorrectly, and accidentally watered the whole batch down. As it simmered, I secretly hoped that eventually the extra water would burn off and things would be fine.

Unfortunately, it didn't work out that way.

While the water seemed to boil down and evaporate, watering it down in the beginning still resulted in ruining the entire pot. The faces in my home were not happy as I nonchalantly slopped a big scoop of soggy, watered-down rice, onto their plates.

Looking back, my first mistake was buying a cheap American version of rice, which can be cooked in less than five minutes, instead of the long-grain Jasmine rice the family prefers. However, I exacerbated the situation by measuring by sight instead of by measuring cup, and watered it down past the point of being edible.

It was just a flavorless, soggy, unappetizing, American version of what should have been a tasty dish. You could still legitimately say that it was rice, but it wasn't all that rice was meant to be.

Food tastes the best when it isn't watered-down. When we more carefully pay attention to a recipe and get all of the elements of a dish measured out to their intended proportions, it becomes not only nutritious, but tasty as well.

Lately I've been thinking that the message of Jesus is a lot like this batch of rice—appetizing and filling in the original form, but completely bland when watered-down and slopped onto our plates by a cook who didn't pay attention to the instructions on the side of the box.

For far too long in contemporary Christian culture we've watered-down the message of Jesus to the point that many people are no longer attracted to it. It's easy to look at these people who push the plate back with a "no thank you" and think that they're refusing the rice altogether. The truth? I think they're just pushing back the soggy, watered-down version we've slung onto their plates—and they would have a completely different reaction if we invited them to taste this meal as intended, instead of our cheap, simmered down, American version.

They're not looking for an American Jesus, they're looking for the real deal. People don't want the watered-down message of Jesus we've been trying to feed them for the past two generations—they're looking for something more authentic, something more applicable, something more…real.

Before we go any further, I imagine there is a chance that the term "watering down the gospel" triggers something in you—it does for me as well. The accusation that some other group or person is "watering down the gospel" is an easy one to make. It's an accusation I've heard many, many times over the years—and have even been on the receiving end of it a time or two. I once wrote a post on my blog at Patheos, which spoke out against violence and oppression and was accused by a reader of preaching a: "liberal, *watered-down*, democratic, toothless and people-pleasing gospel."

The accusation that someone else is watering down the message of Jesus is an accusation we make too freely.

And, if you've been part of American Christianity very long, I'm sure you've heard (or even used) this term as well.

Often when someone else is saying something that sounds a little too loving, a little too inclusive, or a little too _____, we quickly dismiss them by saying they're "watering down the gospel." I've heard the phrase slung a million times in self-serving situations by people who wish to dismiss another's point of view without actually wrestling with the issue at hand. I confess, I've done it myself in the past.

The truth is, I never really knew what this term means. The closest I can come up with is that it's used as a code word for someone being a "liberal." However, the more I think about that batch of rice I ruined, I think a better way of understanding the concept of watering down the message of Jesus is: anything we do that distorts, obscures, or hinders others from experiencing the true taste and flavor of the message of Jesus.

One way of looking at my failed attempt at making rice was that I added too much water. Conversely, I could also argue that I simply forgot to add enough rice. In this way, watering down the message of Jesus isn't exclusively adding in what doesn't belong but also includes neglecting essential elements of the recipe that equally lead to an end product that looks and tastes nothing like the picture we see on the box.

Sometimes we do this unintentionally. With my batch of rice, I *thought* I was getting the recipe correct, yet because I was not paying close attention, the end dish still came out soggy and unappealing. Other times we do this deliberately, purposely skipping an item in the recipe that we simply don't like *(Black olives? No thanks; I'll leave those out)*.

Either way, the end result is...well, less than what the creator of the dish intended for our taste buds to experience.

Growing up in conservative evangelicalism, I was gently led to believe that everyone other than ourselves watered-down the message of Jesus. I remember as a child driving past other churches in the area and asking what made them different from us. When passing the Methodist and Congregational churches, I was told that they were simply "social clubs," and when passing the local Assembly of God I was told that they were "crazy people." A distorted expression of what it means to follow Jesus was always something *they* were doing—never something I or we were doing.

There were always hard lines about who was in and who was out; and conveniently enough, we always managed to be "in." We're often tempted to think that we have it right, and those who are different have it wrong—*it's easy to see someone else as watering down the message of Jesus.*

Herein the problem lies. Yes, there's nothing good about a watered-down, soggy, bland Jesus—but we've got to stop pointing to "the others" as the ones responsible for it, and start turning those fingers inward. Unfortunately, that's not a comfortable process. It's usually much easier to focus on them, not us—you, and not me. Jesus, however, calls us to look *here* before we go searching *there*.

In the Gospel according to Matthew we are told that one day Jesus saw a large crowd of people and decided to go sit on top of a mountain so he could teach them. The sermon that followed has come to be known as the "Sermon on the Mount" and contains some of the richest gems in all the teachings of Jesus. Toward the end of the sermon Jesus teaches with the well-known adage:

> *"Why do you look at the speck of sawdust in your brother's eye and pay no attention to the plank in your own eye? How can you say to your brother, 'Let me take the speck out of your eye,' when all the time there is a plank in your own eye? You hypocrite, first take the plank out of your own eye, and then you will see clearly to remove the speck from your brother's eye"* (Matthew 7:3-5).

It's interesting to see how Jesus describes this idea of focusing on others instead of us. In describing the "others," Jesus uses the term κάρφος to describe their problem—a Greek word that literally means a "splinter." However, when describing the way we should view our own personal shortcomings, Jesus uses the word δοκός which means a "large beam of timber." That's a pretty drastic comparison! With the former in our eye it may be a small nuisance, but if we have the latter in our eyes it could completely blind us from seeing things the way they truly are.

We've got to focus on the beam that is distorting how we see God and others around us.

We've got to remove this, even if taking it out is an uncomfortable, painful process.

To begin removing it, we need to identify and correct the ways in which American Christian culture has promoted a distorted, Americanized Jesus.

We need to undergo a process of undiluting.

Whether we tip the pot to pour some of the water out, or simply add more rice, we need to do something.

If we are to take the teachings of Jesus to heart, we should begin to see the ways we have distorted his radically powerful message as being a massive beam of timber that is completely obstructing our view of who he is—compared to the small splinter, barely visible, in the lives of others.

Let's look inward. Let's discover ways we are watering down the message of Jesus to the point where we are serving up tasteless slop. Let's find the missing ingredients, which, if added as intended, will radically change the flavor of this dish.

The final message of Jesus is called the Great Commission. In the Great Commission, Jesus instructs his disciples to go out and make more disciples. As a result, for the past 2,000 years the Christian faith has been packaged and exported to more and more cultures as the years pass. In principle, this is obviously good. However, one of the challenges that this mission has faced is that the message of Jesus was and is, radically counter-cultural. Yet, instead of allowing the message of Jesus to result in a radical reordering of society, most cultures experience a process of assimilation, where elements of culture blend into the message of Jesus to the point where it is difficult to see where one ends and the other begins.

After a while, the message has a tendency to get diluted.

The message of Jesus then, no longer becomes counter to culture but simply part of culture.

As Americans, we have been well adept at pointing this out in other cultures (such as Christian/Animistic blends in other countries where the message of Jesus has taken root); however, we don't always do an adequate job at identifying such occurrences in our own culture. This becomes a classic case of fish not being aware of the water they are swimming in, as our practice of the message of Jesus becomes blended with culture instead of counter to culture.

Once this process of assimilation takes hold, we end up with all sorts of distorted views about what it means to follow Jesus. The Christian faith begins to look like a nation, a denomination, a political party, or a theological movement.

It starts to look like all sorts of things.

Except for Jesus.

With the founding of the Moral Majority in 1979, theologically conservative Christians were no longer content to live out their faith quietly in their own communities—they wanted to seize political power on a national scale. Many in Christian leadership broke with their own traditions that typically valued the separation of church and state, and began a Christian political movement that would, in many ways, dominate the national discourse for the next 25 years. Since the loudest voices are often the voices that the average person associates with any movement, too many people have been mistakenly convinced that an American political movement is the same thing as the Jesus movement.

People are mistakenly led to believe that American Christian culture is the same thing as Christ himself.

It's not.

In fact, reducing it in these ways, regardless of political or theological persuasion, distorts the message of Jesus.

What was intended to be a beautiful dish, becomes soggy slop.

As a result of this blend between Jesus and culture, many of us have been left with a distorted view of Jesus and what it looks like to follow him. The message of the greatest teacher in all human history, the Son of

God, the awaited Messiah, the Savior of humanity, has had his message reduced to:

- Don't drink.

- Don't smoke.

- Abortion is murder.

- Gay marriage will destroy us.

- Don't forget to vote republican.

This blending of the countercultural teachings of Jesus and contemporary Christian culture has resulted in a damaging obfuscation of the message of Jesus, which is causing people to walk away in droves. Many who don't walk away entirely, are left wandering—seeking something that's more authentic than the watered-down, reduced and distorted, American version.

Recent studies, such as the extensive research conducted by the Barna Group, have revealed that American Christianity has an image crisis—and I believe this image crisis is a result of the assimilation of the teachings of Jesus into Western culture. This image crisis means more and more of the younger generations are opting out of participating in American Christianity as a whole. Many churches throughout the country look out at the sea of faces only to realize that they are old, white congregations, and that they are dying off without having anyone to continue moving it forward.

Some might argue that the current generation seems uninterested in Christianity because they want to avoid issues like sin and repentance, but I don't think that's the case. I think people are hungry for Jesus, but they are starting to realize they have been fed a cheap American version, and they are rightly rejecting this counterfeit. Their rejection should be seen not as a rejection of Jesus, but a rejection of obscured versions of him.

People are tired of being fed a watered-down version of Jesus.

People are tired of an American Jesus.

They want something that's more…

Undiluted.

While some studies are showing that young people are walking away from church and organized Christianity, others are showing that Jesus himself is more popular than ever. There is a quiet spirit slowly awakening in this next generation testifying within them, that the Jesus of scripture is way, way more than what they have experienced being offered in much of American Christian culture.

And, that spirit is correct.

Jesus is way, way more.

While it may be tempting to believe that GenXers and Millennials want less of Jesus, I believe the truth is that they want more of him. Those disillusioned with Christian culture simply long for a more authentic portrait of him.

They just want the real Jesus.

If you're reading this book, I think you do too.

As we press forward, it's important to understand that we have all diluted the message of Jesus in our own ways, whether that has been intentionally or unintentionally. The problem comes when we are always focused on the "other" who is watering down Jesus, instead of ourselves.

We have done it individually, and our culture has done it collectively. For one reason or another, none of us have a completely undiluted understanding of the message of Jesus.

On the intentional side, it's human nature to try to find loopholes in something that seems challenging, difficult, or that we don't want to apply to our individual lives. On the unintentional side, it is equally normal for fish to be completely unaware of the water they are swimming in.

The good news? Both can be fixed.

The solution to bad theology is always good theology. The solution to a watered-down Jesus is a quest to rediscover the undiluted Jesus and the radical elements of his message that so often get lost in our culture. This book will help you reclaim a faith that looks less like American culture, and more like Jesus of Nazareth.

But I must warn you: the process is not always comfortable. We have been thoroughly conditioned to view Jesus through the lenses of our culture—especially American Christian culture. As a result we tend to resist and reject anything that challenges our cultural conditioning. To successfully navigate these waters, you'll need to be willing to set aside whatever culture has told you, and be willing to rediscover the radical message of Jesus.

We must be willing to engage in a lifelong journey of discovering something that, once upon a time, was undiluted.

If you do, you'll find peace.

If you do, you'll find life.

Not just generic peace and generic life—I'm talking about a peace that goes beyond typical human reasoning, and a life that is so abundant it will radically reshape how you view the world around you.

This is a journey…

An uncomfortable, but ridiculously exciting journey.

As I invite you into the personal transformation I experienced during my years at Gordon-Conwell, let's wrestle with the ways we and American Christian culture have diluted and distorted the message of Jesus. Let us uncover a new way of Christian living that is more true to the authentic, wellspring of life and the living waters we find in Jesus of Nazareth.

Let's reclaim a faith that looks less like our culture—and more like Jesus.

CHAPTER 2

Undiluted Reorientation

Yet you refuse to come to me to receive
this life (JOHN 5:40 NLT).

Some days I'm shocked that my wife and I ever got married. We had a miserable courtship characterized by fights and break-ups that looked more like an 8ᵗʰ grade spring romance than it did two people dating in their 30s. She, a Christian therapist, once broke up with me because she said I had too many unresolved childhood issues, and I once broke up with her because I had decided that we weren't spiritually compatible—after all, she refused to admit she was a fundamentalist, said things like "I can't stand Christians," and read authors like Donald Miller—who at the time I was convinced wasn't even really saved. I had some strong beliefs about what it meant to be a Christian (the biggest understatement of this book), and she simply didn't fit the mold.

For one reason or another, we kept coming back to each other. Eventually we decided to make it a permanent situation, and got married twelve weeks later. With all of the back and forth bantering during our courtship and early marriage, one thing remained consistent: Tracy insisted that I needed to go to seminary. I, of course, refused and instead placed my full energy into finding reasons why I shouldn't, or couldn't go. Yet, for more than two solid years Tracy gently (and sometimes not so gently), pushed the issue of going to seminary. With one of the top seminaries in the country (Gordon-Conwell Theological Seminary) just two hours south of where we lived, I at least capitulated into attending a weekend visit to the campus called "Discover Gordon-Conwell."

I enjoyed the campus and meeting the faculty, but after the weekend something just wasn't sitting right in my pure fundamentalist soul. As we hopped in the car and drove back to Maine that rainy April afternoon, I indignantly turned to my wife and said, "They can't possibly be teaching the truth here if they have 100 denominations represented!"

Heresy abounded there, I was sure.

Like being caught up in a Christian version of Alice in Wonderland, Tracy gently encouraged me to put one foot in front of the other and to see just how deep this rabbit hole would go. Reluctantly I filled out the application, and told her that I would go if God removed every barrier, and made it obvious that this was the direction he wanted for my future.

I absolutely did not want to go. Something smelled fishy to me, because a place that had that much theological diversity surely was not of God. However, as one barrier after another was torn down, the picture of my future began to slowly move into my field of vision and increase in its clarity. Eventually, I realized that God had done exactly what I thought he wouldn't do—neutralize all of the excuses I had been using to avoid going.

Unless I was willing to back out of the deal I made with God, Benjamin L. Corey was headed to seminary. After the last barrier was removed, we promptly packed up our house and moved to the quaint city of Beverly in Boston's North Shore. Still nervous about the potential that my mind would be filled with heresy, the only hope I had left was that God would miraculously protect me from any of the heretics who didn't believe in the imminent rapture of the true church.

Seminary, as it turned out, rocked my world.

My first semester was a miserable experience, which left me exhausted and discouraged at the end of each day. As old thought patterns and ways of viewing God were challenged, I began a process of resistance as I tried to hold on to old concepts—a choice that sent me into a considerable depression. For a while, I was ready to go back home and move on to something else, but eventually I decided it wouldn't hurt to simply wrestle with what was being taught, and to give God a little room to show me something new. My new attitude quickly brought me to the place where I began to realize what I had always feared: *I didn't know it all.* What was worse, I also began to accept that some of the things I was taught about God growing up were just plain wrong.

It wasn't an easy place to be in, but I knew this spiritual door could not be shut once it had been cracked open. Much like Neo in the *Matrix,* I had taken the red pill, and there was no turning back...I was on a journey to discover how deep the rabbit hole goes.

Once I gave in and decided to embrace the learning process, the experience of deconstructing, relearning, and paradigm shifts was something I, at least temporarily, found new and exciting. Much like the early stages of a romantic relationship, I was giddy and had butterflies in my stomach a lot of the time. Eventually however, this process began to take a toll on me spiritually. In many cases, I experienced a total collapse of previous paradigms but had nothing yet to replace them with, a situation that is far more frightening than simply replacing an old belief with a new one.

As the newness of my journey wore off, the butterflies turned into fear, and I began to wonder what I had gotten myself into. It wasn't before long that I was facing a crisis of faith. I had come into seminary with an arrogant, know-it-all attitude, and quickly was confronted by how little I knew after all.

I had no idea what to do.

I had no idea what I even believed anymore.

I knew that I wanted to follow Jesus, but everything else seemed up in the air to me. There was no longer a label that applied to me, a denomination I felt compelled to be part of, and there wasn't a movement I wanted to join—I was in no-man's-land.

I was so very lonely. Looking back however, I now realize that God had me right where he wanted me—totally sold out on the idea of following

Jesus, but ready to walk away from all the other nonsense that dilutes the radical message of Jesus.

The loneliness, depression, and fear of no longer being sure what I believed in had me utterly frozen. I felt like a mountaineer who had been overcome with panic halfway up a vertical cliff—too scared to climb any higher, and too scared to crawl back down. No matter how hard I tried, I simply could not find a way to move forward or backward...I was stuck.

At the height of my spiritual despair Tracy and I found ourselves attending a new church, since nothing else seemed to fit us anymore. Within a few weeks of attending our new church, I ended up attending a men's retreat—which in itself was an absolute miracle because I don't do men's retreats. They're too religious, entirely too lame, and I'm always the only guy with earrings and lots of tattoos. But this one, I knew I was supposed to attend.

I was sure of it.

During the retreat I took advantage of the opportunity to have a personal conversation with our new pastor, Joel. He was easy to open up to, close to my age, had also attended Gordon-Conwell, and seemed to be a guy who would be "friendly" to someone disillusioned with American Christianity. As we began to talk, I dumped on him my entire situation—explaining that I was having a crisis of biblical proportions (excuse the pun), because I was attending one of the top seminaries in the country, but had no clue what I believed in anymore.

It wasn't supposed to be this way, I thought.

I explained that I felt more compelled to follow Jesus than ever before, but that I didn't know if I was a Calvinist or an Arminian, a pre-tribber or preterist, or anything else that seminarians were expected to know. I was in no-man's-land, and all I knew was that I really, really wanted to be like Jesus.

It was then that Joel said something that put words to what I was experiencing: "If I'm hearing you correctly, it sounds like you are experiencing a profound reorientation of your faith—not around doctrine or tradition, but simply one that is reoriented on the person of Jesus," he calmly explained.

Joel reassured me that this wasn't a crisis at all—it was actually a beautiful occurrence. God had brought me out of fundamentalism, out of Americanized Christianity, out of black-and-white thinking, out of denominational loyalty, and refocused me simply on the person of Jesus. He reasoned and explained to me that the invitation was never an invitation to follow a tradition or tribe, but was always an invitation to follow Jesus.

My spirit inside knew that what Joel was saying was true: the radical message of Jesus really was that simple.

"Follow *me*," Jesus invites.

I have no idea why it had taken me so long to realize that the missing piece of my faith was Jesus himself. Sure, Jesus was part of it. Sometimes he might even be the center of it, *but he was never all of it.* No matter what nice language was used to describe it, it was never a faith that was boiled down to following Jesus—it was diluted with too much other garbage.

All along I had been living a diluted faith watered-down with labels, loyalty to tradition, loyalty to a "movement"—loyalty to a lot of things other than Jesus. As a result, I came to realize the faith that had been set on the table before me, wasn't appetizing at all, because the true flavor was masked by too many labels and too many theological traditions.

You see, if we want to live a faith that isn't diluted to the point of mush, it needs to be a faith that is totally and completely centered on Jesus—and nothing else. It can *include* other things, but cannot be *centered* on anything else. We must be willing to tip the pot over and pour out anything that is detracting from the centrality of Christ—even if that means dumping some long-held belief systems, or adding ones that we forgot to add to the pot.

Reorienting our faith on Jesus will also mean that we become willing to reject many concepts about what it means to follow Jesus—even if that means dumping stuff that comes from American Christian culture. We'll have to relearn that it's not about whether or not we are a Calvinist or an Arminian, it's not about whether we are Charismatic, Protestant, Catholic, or an Anabaptist...

The only question that really matters is: are we people who actually look like Jesus?

I've been invited to follow a lot of traditions, a lot of movements, and to follow a lot of particular doctrines, but I've rarely had people simply invite me to follow Jesus. Unfortunately, regardless of which tradition, movement, or doctrine faith is oriented upon—regardless of whether or not the traditions or doctrines are good and correct—such a faith becomes a spiritual parasite that slowly drains the life force from within. It can be sustained for a time, but in the end brings about spiritual death.

Thankfully, Jesus doesn't invite us into a rigid religion, a tiresome tradition, or loyalty to a black-and-white set of doctrines—Jesus simply invites us to get up and follow in his footsteps.

When we encounter Jesus in the New Testament calling his first disciples, we don't see him passing out a lengthy statement of faith, church constitutions, or bylaws—we simply find him offering the invitation to put down whatever weight we have been carrying for too long, and follow him.

> *"Come, **follow me**," Jesus said, "and I will send you out to fish for people." At once they left their nets and **followed him** (Matthew 4:19-20).*

> *Jesus called them, and immediately they left the boat and their father and **followed him** (Matthew 4:21-22).*

> *But Jesus told him, "**Follow me**, and let the dead bury their own dead" (Matthew 8:22).*

> *As Jesus went on from there, he saw a man named Matthew sitting at the tax collector's booth. "**Follow me**," he told him, and Matthew got up and **followed him** (Matthew 9:9).*

> *If you refuse to take up your cross and **follow me**, you are not worthy of being mine (Matthew 10:38 NLT).*

Then Jesus said to his disciples, "If any of you wants to be my **follower,** *you must turn from your selfish ways, take up your cross, and* **follow me** (Matthew 16:24 NLT).

Jesus told him, "If you want to be perfect, go and sell all your possessions and give the money to the poor, and you will have treasure in heaven. Then come, **follow me**" (Matthew 19:21 NLT).

When we look at the undiluted, radical message of Jesus, we see that it was never about wearing a theological label, subscribing to a particular theological structure, or even about becoming a Christian. The undiluted message of Jesus is, and always has been, a straightforward invitation to follow him, and to learn to be like him.

Those who were willing to let go of long-held beliefs in exchange for the words of Jesus experienced a radical new life that accomplished no less than changing the world. Those who didn't? Jesus warned them that he alone was the source of life, and rejecting him in favor of anything, including religion, is to choose that which will spiritually dehydrate instead of that which can breathe new life into dry bones.

The first step in rediscovering the radical message of Jesus is to embrace an undiluted reorientation of our lives on the person and teachings of Jesus Christ. Our starting point in this change of heart must be the realization that the entire Bible is ultimately a book that was designed to point us to Jesus. Whether the writings of Moses or the writings of Paul, these texts are designed for the primary purpose of redirecting our lives back to Jesus—and redirecting us only to Jesus.

In John chapter 5, we find Jesus teaching to a group of highly educated religious conservatives who were experts on scripture—these were the folks who would win a sword drill at church camp every time, even beating out the camp counselors assigned to them. However, Jesus issues a sharp rebuke—claiming that while they know scripture in every respect, they had missed the point that all scripture is designed to point us to him.

You search the Scriptures because you think they give you eternal life. But the Scriptures point to me! Yet you refuse to come to me to receive this life (John 5:39-40 NLT).

We do that too, don't we?

When we find Jesus saying something that sounds a little too radical, a little too merciful, a little to hippie-ish, we look for ways to explain it away. Usually we'll start flipping the pages backward or forward until we find another author who seems to take a different stance from Jesus—one that feels a bit more reasonable to us, and we run with it.

Until we let go and reorient our lives simply on Jesus, we have a tendency to miss the forest from the trees, becoming people of the book but not exactly the people who are trying to look like Jesus. If we want to rediscover the radical message of Jesus and experience a reorientation of our lives, we must become willing to let go of whatever else might be getting in the way—even if that's a religious tradition named after Jesus—and return to the timeless invitation to simply become a follower of him.

The original, radical message was actually quite simple. It was an invitation to walk away from religious burdens, cultural burdens, and old understandings of God, in exchange for following the one who claimed to be the undiluted way, the undiluted truth, and the undiluted life.

In Matthew chapter 7, Jesus warns us of the dangers of orientating our lives on anyone or anything other than him:

Therefore everyone who hears these words of mine and puts them into practice is like a wise man who built his house on the rock. The rain came down, the streams rose, and the winds blew and beat against that house; yet it did not fall, because it had its foundation on the rock. But everyone who hears these words of mine and does not put them into practice is like a foolish man who built his house on sand. The rain came down, the streams rose, and the winds blew and beat against that house, and it fell with a great crash (Matthew 7:24-27).

Jesus says that the ones who reorient their lives in order to make his words, his teachings, and his example their foundational center are wise. Making anything else our foundation or starting point, Jesus claims, is foolish—even if that's a well-meaning religious tradition.

When we refuse to clean house, hit the reset button, and rebuild a faith that is centered solely on Jesus alone, we settle for soggy slop instead of the radiant message he divinely crafted. We become the conservative religious leaders of old, who knew everything the scriptures had to say about God, but completely missed out on experiencing him.

"...Yet you refuse to come to me to receive this life," Jesus warns.

I think what Jesus is warning us about is that it's entirely possible to be a religious, dedicated Christian, and yet totally miss the life-giving nature of a life centered squarely on his teachings. Some of us have exchanged Jesus for a Christian religion.

You've met those people, haven't you?

Well-meaning Christians who are completely dedicated to the Christian religion...but who, for some reason, don't look much like Jesus.

They're all around you, aren't they?

But what if I challenged you to consider something deeper...to consider that *there's actually a chance that you and I might be part of that group.* You and I might actually be fish who are completely unaware of the cultural waters we're swimming in. You and I might actually be more centered on religious tradition, doctrine, or other labels that don't always look like Jesus.

There's a good chance we both are, to some degree.

But, we don't have to be.

If we want to be a people who live an authentic Christlike faith, one that isn't diluted, soggy, and tasteless, we must become a people who radically reorientate our lives on the invitation to drop what we're carrying and just follow him.

The weight that's in your arms right now...it's heavy, isn't it?

The dogma.

The tradition.

The theological labels.

The long list of dos and don'ts.

Like with his first disciples, Jesus has rolled up on the scene and found us to be carrying a lot of nets too. These nets grow so very heavy. So heavy sometimes that we see Jesus slip off into the horizon because we're trying to carry so much that we can't keep up with him even though we intend to.

I know it is, because I have been there.

Jesus knows it is too, and he's inviting you to set it all down beside you so you can simply follow him...

Without getting stuck in the bushes behind.

> *Then Jesus said, "Come to me, all of you who are weary and carry heavy burdens, and I will give you rest. Take my yoke upon you. Let me teach you, because I am humble and gentle at heart, and you will find rest for your souls. For my yoke is easy to bear, and the burden I give you is light"* (Matthew 11:28-30 NLT).

If the way you're living is sucking the life out of you, let me encourage you to consider that it might be this way because you have yet to experience a radical reorientation of your faith around the person and teachings of Jesus.

You might be trying to move in the direction of Jesus, but perhaps you're trying to maintain so many nets in your arms, that Jesus always seems to be off in the distance somewhere.

If we're not only to rediscover the radical message of Jesus, but actually experience it too, we need to set aside these nets—even if someone has spray painted the name of Jesus on them. We must hit the reset button, become like children again, and reorientate ourselves on a faith that is focused on living out the words and example of Jesus.

We need to become like the wise man, and stop living like the foolish one.

When we make this change, Jesus promises that it's a light load to carry. A faith that has an undiluted reorientation on him is not burdensome and actually leads to new life.

It's time to lay down tradition, theological labels, reliance on denominational identity, and anything else that is providing a foundation deeper than Jesus himself. While culture places high value on tribal identity, Jesus simply says, "If you want to put down your nets, you can come follow me. We don't really have a name for ourselves, but I will show you the best way to live."

It's time to put down our nets, and trade them for a life that invites us to freely follow Jesus.

It's time to tip the pot over and pour out everything except the rice, and start over from there.

If we embrace an undiluted reorientation, we just might find that Jesus was telling the truth when he said he was "the way" and that he was "the life."

CHAPTER 3

Undiluted Community

...stay awake with me
(MATTHEW 26:38 THE LIVING BIBLE).

As I reorientated my life simply on Jesus and began actually trying to follow him, I quickly realized that this would be a lonely and impossible endeavor if I tried to do this alone. Shutting out the inner voices that told me I should strive for spiritual strength through independence wasn't easy, but I knew that if I was going to make it very far on this path, I couldn't walk alone. There was a time and a place for priding myself in independence and my own ability, but I knew following Jesus wasn't it.

From our earliest years, American culture reinforces the notion that we are all completely independent individuals. Sometimes we call it "personal responsibility" and other times we call it "rugged individualism," which, in and of themselves, are not entirely negative concepts. Taken too far however, these cultural concepts lead us to believe we really are the captains of our own ship, that our primary responsibility is to our own selves, and that we can do this all on our own.

But, we are not.

And, we can't.

Our culture idolizes the concept of a "self-made man," tells us that we must be primarily "true to ourselves," and having an "independent

personality" is generally seen as a strength. Culture tells us these things…
but the message of Jesus does not.

With the powerful waters of culture surrounding us from the
moment of birth, we unintentionally end up with a faith that is often
more influenced by aspects of the culture around us than a faith rooted
in the undiluted, radical message of Jesus. As we live out a faith that is
blindly infused with an individualistic culture, we end up with a distorted approach to faith that leaves us lonely, isolated, and alone.

In order to not only rediscover the radical message of Jesus, but in
order to actually have a shot at living this out in an authentic way, we must
return to the truth discovered in God's original plan for humanity—we
need to return to the beginning. In returning to the beginning, we are able
to see that we were not made to be completely independent as culture too
often teaches us, but instead were designed to live in undiluted community
with others—something reaffirmed in the radical message of Jesus.

The Creation Poem of Genesis 1 tells a beautiful story of the God who
masterfully created everything. The author of Genesis goes on to tell us
that when God finished with the process of creation he stepped back, had
a good look, and pronounced that all of it was "good."

God created light…and God saw that it was good.

God separated land from the sea…and God saw that it was good.

God created vegetation…and God saw that it was good.

God created the sun and the moon…and God saw that it was good.

God created the animals of the seas…and God saw that it was good.

God created the animals of the land…and God saw that it was good.

God created humanity…and God saw that it was good.

Clearly God was happy with everything he created, and pronounced
every single part of it to be "good." However, God had yet to create a second human; Adam was completely alone. God notices this and in Genesis
2, when he looked at a single human being living alone, outside the context
of community, we finally hear God say something he hadn't said before:

"It's not good to be alone," God pronounces.

God knew it wouldn't be healthy for Adam to live life on his own, outside of community with others. That, God said, would not be good. To rectify the situation God created the first community of two, and invited them to experience life together in intimate and meaningful ways. Seeing that community, relationships, and an authentic sharing of life with others to be good and beautiful, God actually commands them to go out and *make even more community,* together.

Living life as an individual apart from authentic and intimate communal relationships was never part of the deal. From the first humans created, God created us to be communal beings who crave, and actually need, to live life in the context of authentic, interdependent relationships with others.

We were created for community.

We even see that *God himself* wanted "in" when it came to this new community, as he took afternoon walks with them during the cool part of the day—building and participating in community *with* them. God even went looking for them when he realized the relationship had been damaged and needed restoration, as one does in the context of authentic, communal relationships.

From the very beginning we were created not for rugged individualism and independence, but for community with others. As we rediscover the radical message of Jesus, we find that he reaffirms not our cultural appreciation for individualism, but God's original plan that we do life in the context of community.

When Jesus arrives on the scene, he finds himself in the middle of heated cultural debates on how to interpret and apply scripture within his cultural context (sound familiar?). Two leading rabbis of the first century, Hillel and Shammai, had sparked two different schools of thought on contemporary ethics in Hebrew culture—quite similar to the right vs. left polarization we experience in our own culture. When we find Jesus being asked questions in the Gospels, what we often are seeing from a historical perspective is the crowd attempting to see which camp he sides with.

One of the common issues debated between the House of Hillel and the House of Shammai was the question of divorce. The House of Shammai held a more rigid interpretation of the law, arguing that it was only permissible to divorce your spouse for a serious wrongdoing such as unfaithfulness. The House of Hillel, on the other hand, famously argued that it was permissible to divorce over any issue that one found remotely displeasing—such as being a bad cook.

And so in Matthew 19, we find Jesus being asked by the religious leaders which side he is on—that of Hillel or that of Shammai. In this particular case, Jesus ends up siding with Shammai. What is beautiful about the way Jesus chooses to weigh in on this debate is that he goes beyond the question and returns us to the beginning—reminding us that we were created to live in unbroken community.

As usual, instead of answering the question in a straightforward way, Jesus goes deeper than the question itself:

"For this reason a man will leave his father and mother and be united to his wife, and the two will become one flesh," Jesus reminds them.

As with many of the other statements of Jesus, our culture often causes us to miss the beauty of this passage because it's far easier to read in our current cultural and theological debates and miss the core of what he is teaching. Jesus isn't making a political statement about how he thinks secular governments should define marriage—what he is alluding to is much, much more profound and applicable. He's actually making a statement about living in unbroken community, even when it's just a community of two.

And so, Jesus takes them back to the beginning: "Living in unbroken community was always the plan," he essentially says.

We were created as relational beings for the purpose of enjoying community with the divine, and one of the primary ways God intended that to be experienced was in and through authentic, intimate relationships with other people. Our ability to most fully experience the divine is directly linked to our ability to most fully experience relationships with other human beings.

One without the other is not the undiluted life in community God created us to experience.

Someone once asked Gandhi for a sermon, and his reply was, "My life is my sermon." In the same way, we see how Jesus chose to live his adult life as perhaps one of his most potent sermons of all. While our contemporary Christian culture places value on the unholy trinity of buildings, bodies, and bucks, Jesus—the wisest teacher who ever lived and central figure in human history—was a homeless man who instead lived his life investing in authentic community with twelve close friends. We see them wrestle with the radical nature of his message together, share meals together, serve the poor and hungry together, and share life's burdens with one another.

It is easy for us to look at the gospel narrative and mistakenly see Jesus and his disciples as simply a traveling teacher with his traveling students—but the story is much more than that. Throughout their time together we see that this was a mutual, two-way community, with Jesus not only leading his disciples, but serving them as well, as we see him gently wash their dusty feet. We find Jesus not only comforting and sharing the burdens of his disciples, but also asking them to share *his own burdens* as well. In fact, on the last night of his life, we see Jesus practically beg them to sit up and keep him company during his darkest hours—as fear and anxiety over the future nearly overwhelmed him.

The Son of God himself did not want to bear the burdens of life outside the context of relationship with others.

Can we wrap our heads around that for a minute?

Jesus, the Son of God, was able to walk on water, make food appear out of thin air, was able to liven up a party with the water-to-wine miracle, told a storm to knock it off (and the storm listened); he was able to make lame people walk, blind people see, deaf people hear—even putting a severed ear back on a person, and even told a man who had been dead four days to wake up (and he did!).

But there is one thing that Jesus didn't do, and didn't want to do. Jesus didn't want to experience the ups and downs of life outside the context of close, authentic relationships. Jesus, the second member of the trinity who created the entire universe, needed a community of close friends with whom to share his burdens.

The radical message of Jesus tells that that not even God wants to live outside of authentic community with others.

That's crazy.

So, the question we need to start asking becomes: if Jesus himself needed to live out his faith in the context of community, why do we so often fool ourselves into thinking we can do it alone?

The life of Jesus teaches us many things, but among the most important is that the best way to live life is not through a hyper-focus on individualism or independency, but through a conscious decision to share our lives, openly and authentically, with those around us. He teaches us that we must not only be served—but must serve others. He teaches that we aren't to simply share other people's burdens but should allow the weight of our own burdens to be spread out as well. Jesus teaches us that a life best lived, is a life lived together.

The early church seemed to nail it when it came to living out the sermon of Jesus' life. Throughout the book of Acts (the book in the Bible that records the activities of the earliest Christians), we find they not only lived communally with each other, but that they actually took it to extremes that would make many an American Christian uncomfortable.

These early Christians had a strong sense of community, often meeting in small, house churches—a practice that facilitated deeper intimacy as they wrestled with this new faith, together. In addition to exploring their faith in a relational way, they also put undiluted community into practice by rejecting the concept of individual ownership in lieu of an "according to need, according to ability" redistribution of wealth system—a practice that enabled them to eradicate poverty in their community:

No one claimed that any of their possessions was their own, but they shared everything they had. ...And God's grace was so powerfully at work in them all that there were no needy persons among them. For from time to time those who owned land or houses sold them, brought the money from the sales and put it at the apostles' feet, and it was distributed to anyone who had need (Acts 4:32-35).

The early Christians didn't have megachurches where people watched a pastor with a $250,000 salary preach via a Jumbotron from a satellite campus; they didn't "worship" beside people they'd seen several times before but never actually met, and they didn't preach a hyper-capitalistic, American version of Christianity. The first Christians lived in the context of community and wrestled with an emerging theology among a tight-knit group of friends—friends who shared every aspect of their lives together, including their wealth.

They did life together, in every respect.

The undiluted version looked a lot different from American versions of Christianity.

Western, individualistic culture invites us to embrace our independence and champion our ability to do this all on our own, but the life of Jesus invites us to embrace a healthy interdependency on others. The radical message of Jesus invites us to express and wrestle with our faith in a lifestyle of unbroken community with others. In Western culture however, living in community often is against the flow of how our society works. As culture has morphed deeper and deeper into a strictly individualistic-oriented culture, we now find ourselves in a world where it is not uncommon to not even know the name of our neighbors in the house next to us. What's even scarier is that we might not even know the person sitting in the church *pew* next to us.

Sadly, what we often experience is a diluted version of the real thing— we've slowly assimilated our faith to our culture and traded in something designed for the top shelf in exchange for a cheap, less potent knockoff.

Independent, secluded living, hyper-individualized worldviews, and trying to do life on our own, dilutes the experience Jesus intends for us.

But lives that are authentic, transparent, and embrace a circle of meaningful, deep relationships?

That's the undiluted version.

Once you taste this, you quickly come to realize that it tastes way, way better than any version you've tried before.

Looking back to my first year at Gordon-Conwell, loneliness was the most common emotion I remember experiencing. I was new in town without any close friends; I was new to seminary—living off campus, and I was looking for a new church. On top of being new in town and knowing very few people, I was also experiencing a massive paradigm shift in regard to my faith—I knew what I was coming out of, but didn't have a clue what I was moving into. As my old paradigm continued to crumble, I felt even more alienated with the realization that I was daily looking less and less like my old tribe, and didn't have a new one to go to yet. My list of friends was growing smaller, and I knew that I desperately needed to find a community where I could be authentic and wrestle with my faith, safely.

My wife and I quickly learned that true community really is countercultural, and it is not easy to find or build. After trying a few different churches, we ended up at a large mainstream church that had an outstanding preacher. However, after a few months went by, we realized that the church was so large we hadn't seen the same people twice—and didn't know a soul. Church had become a passive experience instead of a relational one. We were singing worship songs with over 1,000 other people, but still felt like we were the only ones in the room.

In an effort to be part of a community, we eventually joined a small group in hopes that would finally quench our thirst—but it didn't. The group was full of wonderful people, but ultimately it became a simple Bible study. A Bible study group, in and of itself, is *not* community. Our weekly conversations were characterized by *"What did that verse mean to you?"* and *"Let's read something by John MacArthur,"* instead of the *"My life is total bullshit right now, and I'm not even sure if I believe this stuff anymore"* conversation that actually would have been beneficial and life-giving. We finally tried to shock the group into going deeper by one night announcing: *"Our marriage sucks right now, and not a person in this room knows that,"* but the silence and blank stares in response told us all we needed to know...so we moved on.

Ultimately the beauty I discovered is that you don't have to find a single community that fits you—you can simply plug into community where you find others doing it. I found safe and authentic community happening in a few different places—places where we could openly wrestle with our faith, where we could be as authentic as we were ready to be, and where we didn't have to be a carbon copy of anyone else in order to be part of it. It was like nothing I had previously tasted in my former version of Christianity, and as soon as I had a sip, I wanted more.

If you look hard and are willing to help build it by being a participant and not a simple observer, you can find and create community—because community happens where you do it.

It's worth it, because good community with authentic people, who value your sacred space, can be spiritually intoxicating.

Meeting my friend Jeff from the Boston Emergent Cohort was one of the best things that ever happened to me. We had connected through a seminary course I was taking on Emergent Theology, and he invited me to an Emergent Cohort event to meet the others. The drive with him into the city from the North Shore took about an hour, and by the time we arrived at the meeting I realized we naturally engaged in raw and intimate conversation about faith, the emotional crisis my paradigm shift was causing, what theologies I was no longer sure of, and even was able to listen to his friend Cynthia talk from the backseat about her program for children with disabilities in Africa. Aside from reassuring me a few times that his car was a "cuss-friendly zone," when I let a few f-bombs slip through, he largely listened, acknowledged, and affirmed that all the things I was wrestling with were legitimate and valid things to struggle with.

For the first time in a year, I felt normal.

And heard.

And energized.

As Jeff introduced me to the Emergent community in the Boston area, my spiritual life had its own great awakening and led me to all sorts of divine encounters where God shaped me in the context of community. Whether it was walking around the city of Salem at Halloween dressed as monks and offering people free blessings (opposed to the hatred they countered from the street preachers who flock to Salem every October), sharing good conversation about God and a midnight Welsh beer in the church sanctuary at the Gathering with my friend, Pastor Phil, or finding myself inspired by the countless people I encountered who were intent on following Jesus while engaging in meaningful social action—I found a broad community of people who got what it was like to authentically live life together.

Finding community where being me was okay, where my sacred space was respected, and where I didn't have to have it all figured out, saved me.

I was starting to catch a glimpse of what undiluted community actually looks like.

The spark that started with Jeff began to fuel a wildfire that would lead to a passion for living in authentic community. A year later my wife and I found ourselves sitting in Chris and Melissa Chang's living room—testing the waters again with a Community Life Group from the church where I had met Joel, who you met earlier. We decided to throw all our cards on the table in the first meeting to make sure we didn't invest in something that wasn't going to be authentic, real community. We let it be known that we were the people who might blurt out something that could potentially take their evening from lighthearted to uncomfortable silence in under three seconds, and that if this was just another Bible study where we might have to filter ourselves while only wading in the shallow end, we weren't interested.

Instead of the socially awkward stares we were prepared for, we were embraced, prayed with, and welcomed into a growing community of friends who would later become a lifeline during the most painful and challenging chapter of our lives. The group shared weekly meals with each other, wrestled with the radical nature of Jesus' message together, laughed together during lighthearted moments, cried together during miscarriages and good-byes, and eventually grew so big that we birthed a whole new community...who did the same things together.

Once you taste undiluted community, it's hard to go back to whatever the watered-down American knockoff would be. Once you realize that you don't have to hold it all together on your own, that you can rely on others, share with others, and be real with others, it's really hard to imagine going back to old ways of doing life.

The radical idea of living in community with a wide range of transparent and authentic relationships is something that gets lost in plastic, throw-away versions of Christianity, and causes us to live a diluted version of the abundant life Jesus promised in John 10:10. However, if we want to rediscover the radical message of Jesus, we must rediscover the radical practice of living in community with others.

Because that's what he did.

Although building community is hard, uncomfortable, and requires vulnerability in a culture that tends to value pretentiousness, the life you will discover at the end of that road is one that you'll never want to turn away from. Like Jesus, we find life as it was intended when we build a circle of friends who will join us in the messy work of wrestling with what faith in our time looks like.

Are you tired of trying to do this on your own? Tired of a bland faith?

When you rediscover the radical message of Jesus, you find that undiluted community might just be the missing element you're searching for.

CHAPTER 4

Undiluted Inclusion

*...people from everywhere kept coming
to him* (MARK 1:45 NLT).

One of the things I grew to love the most about the undiluted communities I had found—whether it was the Boston Emergent Cohort, my friends at The Gathering, the Chang's, or Vida Real (a life group I eventually cofounded with our friends Sarah and Karlos)—was that everyone was welcomed to come and find a safe place to connect to God. Past experiences, I realized, were not community experiences at all but simply ruthless tribalism seeking to conform and convert instead of welcoming the outsider and creating safe spaces to facilitate connection to God and each other.

As I grew to experience and understand what it meant to live in undiluted community, and as I continued to rediscover the radical message of Jesus, I began to not only see God in new ways, and myself in new ways, I began to see others in new ways as well. For the first time in my life, I was beginning to live out my faith in the context of community with people who were not carbon copies of one another, but really quite diverse. What was even stranger was that for the first time in my life, I was no longer feeling the need or desire to condemn those who had different theology, worldviews, or even lifestyles; but instead I began to see them as people who, just like me, needed a safe place to experience God. In time, I even realized that I could learn from them.

Prior to my arrival at Gordon-Conwell and my subsequent reorientation, I had come from a hybrid experience of conservative evangelicalism and legalistic fundamentalism. During my time being indoctrinated in the latter, it was continually drilled into my head that the gospel of Jesus was "offensive," and was something that would earn a faithful Christian a predictable level of persecution throughout life. The gospel, we were taught, will radically offend one's senses, because "broad is the road to destruction and many will find it, but narrow is the way to life and few find it." Offensive, because the lines are drawn in such a way that a select few get in, while most everyone else, is out. Preaching this broad versus narrow paradigm, we were told, would be controversial and offensive because of the exclusive nature of Jesus—it leaves out those who we might think should be let in, and leaves the door cracked for just the few chosen.

I remember sitting in a chapel in Schroon Lake, New York, one fall evening in 1994, for a hell, fire, and brimstone "come to Jesus and repent of not being a virgin" type evening service at Bible School. By the end of the service, many of the non-virgin girls were weeping—not out of repentance, but out of shame. The girl sitting next to me had curly brown hair, a roundish face, and a soft smile, but couldn't stop weeping. Clearly, she wasn't a virgin anymore and until that service, didn't realize how worthless she had become as a result.

These folks consistently reminded us that evening that the gospel of Jesus is supposed to offend people in this way. As the service drew to a close, one of the slightly older Resident Advisors took this girl outside to give her a hug and console her, while the angry man in the suit on stage reminded us that following Jesus would look like what we had seen that evening—that it would be in-your-face offensive, and that many people would walk away because of this confrontational, exclusive nature of Christ. I still recall the way they prompted us about what life would be like when we finally went back home: "Don't worry, when you get home you won't have to leave your friends—your friends are going to be the ones to leave you."

This mindset stuck with me for many years—even long after I had "thought" I rejected these teachings and moved on. Jesus, to me, had become a figure of exclusion who drew hard lines in the sand about who was in and who was out. The worldview I adapted from this indoctrination was that the religious conservatives who rigorously keep the law were the ones who found the narrow road, and that everyone else was hopelessly lost on the broad road of destruction.

As it turns out, I was wrong about Jesus.

Way, way, way wrong.

As I navigated my way through seminary, eventually capitulating to the truth that I knew very little about Jesus, I began to rediscover a man who in some ways was similar to what I had previously thought, but at the same time, was radically different. I began to study the stories of Jesus as if I had never read them before, and realized Jesus looked nothing like the fiery preachers I was used to—Jesus was actually the kind of bloke who would invite me to come over and have a few beers with him. Instead of a man of harsh words, I rediscovered that Jesus was the guy who said, "God didn't send me to condemn the world, but to save it," "neither do I condemn you," and "a new commandment I give you: love each other"—all sayings of Jesus that for whatever reason didn't get much airplay in my old life.

The exclusive Jesus I met at Bible school wasn't the same Jesus I experienced at seminary. Jesus wasn't an in-your-face bully, and he actually wasn't offensive or harsh, unless you were a conservative religious leader.

To everyone else, Jesus was quite kind, really.

The more I read, the more I studied, and the more open I became to embracing a new Jesus and a new Christianity, the more I realized that my previous paradigm had been based on a diluted version of Jesus. In this diluted version, the message of Jesus was good news for a few, and really, really bad news for most of the others. However, the one element from my old paradigm that did carry over into the new is that the message of Jesus is in fact, shocking and offensive. However, the offensiveness comes by totally different reasons from what I had been taught.

The truth I came to see, as was once said by Rachel Held Evans, is that the message of Jesus isn't offensive because of who gets left out, but who gets let in. It's not the exclusivity of the gospel, which is an affront to our sense of justice, but the inclusivity that shocks us—as it did with the religious leaders of Jesus' time. Jesus began and ended his public ministry the same way: by infuriating the religious conservatives through preaching a radical message that included the excluded and embraced the outcast. The first time Jesus does this, it nearly gets him killed—the second time, it actually does.

Not exactly a picture of the Jesus so many of us grow up with, but it's true.

In Luke 4 we stumble upon the story of Jesus preaching his first public sermon. Scripture tells us that he read from the Isaiah scroll—proclaiming that the time had come to speak up for people who were being oppressed—and for a moment, the audience was cool with it all. After some platitudes about what a great preacher he was, Jesus declares that he wasn't actually sent for the people who thought they were "in" but instead came for the people who had long been considered "out." Let's just say that this didn't exactly go over well with the audience; they promptly took him to the edge of town so they could throw him off a cliff.

Those in Jesus' audience would have been filled with nationalistic pride and the notion that they were God's "chosen people," and expected that the long-awaited Messiah would share the same sentiments. The Messiah, they thought, was to come for the "in," not for the "out"; the Messiah was coming for "us" instead of for "them" as well. When Jesus announces a seemingly backward paradigm that focuses on the excluded and exalts the outsider, it infuriates the audience to the point of sparking off a small riot.

The first sermon of Jesus was offensive—not because of who it left out, but because of who it let in. Not because of who got excluded, but because of who got included. The entire ministry of Jesus follows this same pattern of including the excluded and reversing the understanding of "out" versus "in"—a pattern that placed Jesus at constant odds with the religious conservatives of his time.

The undiluted, inclusive Jesus of scripture looks radically different from the diluted, exclusive Jesus we often encounter.

One of the things that most captivates me about Jesus as I read the Gospels is that almost everyone seems drawn to him. The outsiders of the culture long to spend time with him, following from town to town to listen to his parables. Even the cultural elite—the religious leaders, still seem drawn to him and can be consistently seen in the back of a crowd tossing out questions to him. However, the religious leaders always seem to have an ulterior motive when questioning Jesus, something he repeatedly rebukes them for—telling them to "repent." The cultural outsiders on the other hand, those seen as too sinful, too unclean, and too whatever, become Jesus' undiluted community.

Those who fit in neatly at church, those who are hyper-focused on the "law" are told to repent, but the sinners, tax collectors, and prostitutes are invited to sit down for dinner, to share a glass of wine, and to build a friendship. Surely there must have been something so gentle and loving about Jesus that caused those considered the vilest of society to pull up a chair, pour a tall glass, and strike up a friendship. While as a teenager I had been taught that living for Jesus means all your friends will abandon you, at seminary I started looking at the real Jesus and discovered he was actually so popular that one could argue he lived with the thorn of celebrity status.

> As a result, large crowds soon surrounded Jesus, and he couldn't publicly enter a town anywhere. He had to stay out in the secluded places, but people from everywhere kept coming to him (Mark 1:45 NLT).

Jesus, it appears, was actually a likable and popular guy—not at all the angry and disliked version of Jesus that was painted for me back at Bible school all those years back.

Unfortunately, Jesus and the religious conservatives of his day never seem to hit it off, because Jesus is always busy making friends with the outcasts and completely reversing the lines of who was in and who was out. To the religious elite, the message of Jesus became progressively offensive; to the morally flawed seekers, the poor, and the outcast however, it became the best news they had ever heard. As a result, the religious leaders continually tried to discredit Jesus—calling him a "drunkard and a glutton" because in their eyes he had shared too many meals and too many glasses of wine with the worst of sinners (Matthew 11:19).

Dietrich Bonhoeffer once argued that the church isn't truly the church until and unless it exits for the "other." This sentiment of inclusion of the "other" is something we see building throughout the ministry of Jesus— and something we as Jesus followers should pay close attention to. More and more directly, Jesus taught and demonstrated a radical inclusion that systematically infuriated the religious teachers who kept tabs on him.

Many who follow Jesus throughout his ministry are continually shocked by his inclusion of the "other" and how radically expansive Jesus is in defining the "other." In the book of Matthew we find Jesus flipping the old paradigm on a few occasions. First, Jesus announces in Matthew 7 that there are plenty of people who sound religious and publically confess Jesus is Lord, but still refuse to embrace living in the Kingdom of God— flipping the old paradigm of keepers of the law being in and the moral failures being out. He goes further in Matthew 8 to confront common misperceptions of his time, as it was commonly believed that the Jews had a special "in-ness" but that Gentiles were "out." Jesus tells the crowds that the "other" we often think is "out" actually has a seat at God's table.

> *And I tell you this, that many Gentiles will come from all over the world—from east and west—and sit down with Abraham, Isaac, and Jacob at the feast in the Kingdom of Heaven. But many Israelites—those for whom the Kingdom was prepared—will be thrown into outer darkness, where there will be weeping and gnashing of teeth* (Matthew 8:11-12 NLT).

Further along, Jesus begins working his radical message of inclusion into his parables. This keys us into the importance of his message of inclusion; as parables invited hearers to wrestle with the message, and slowly begin gleaning truth from the story. When Jesus conveys a message via a parable, it can be a good sign that it is an especially important truth because he chooses to teach it in such a way that forces you to think long and hard about it.

One day in Jesus' ministry he is found teaching on the issue of humility and teaches his disciples ways they might show humility in practical situations, such as when attending a wedding banquet. However, when someone from the crowd speaks up and says that attending a banquet in the Kingdom of God will be a wonderful experience, Jesus jumps on the opportunity to work his message of inclusion of the "other" into his lesson.

Jesus replied with this story: "A man prepared a great feast and sent out many invitations. When the banquet was ready, he sent his servant to tell the guests, 'Come, the banquet is ready.' But they all began making excuses. One said, 'I have just bought a field and must inspect it. Please excuse me.' Another said, 'I have just bought five pairs of oxen, and I want to try them out. Please excuse me.' Another said, 'I now have a wife, so I can't come.'

"The servant returned and told his master what they had said. His master was furious and said, 'Go quickly into the streets and alleys of the town and invite the poor, the crippled, the blind, and the lame.' After the servant had done this, he reported, 'There is still room for more.' So his master said, 'Go out into the country lanes and behind the hedges and urge anyone you find to come, so that the house will be full. For none of those I first invited will get even the smallest taste of my banquet'" (Luke 14:16-24 NLT).

Later, Jesus tells yet another parable to illustrate that plenty of people are in even though it seems radically unfair to religious conservatives who think they have a monopoly on in-ness:

> *"For the Kingdom of Heaven is like the landowner who went out early one morning to hire workers for his vineyard. He agreed to pay the normal daily wage and sent them out to work.*
>
> *"At nine o'clock in the morning he was passing through the marketplace and saw some people standing around doing nothing. So he hired them, telling them he would pay them whatever was right at the end of the day. So they went to work in the vineyard. At noon and again at three o'clock he did the same thing.*
>
> *"At five o'clock that afternoon he was in town again and saw some more people standing around. He asked them, 'Why haven't you been working today?'*
>
> *"They replied, 'Because no one hired us.'*
>
> *"The landowner told them, 'Then go out and join the others in my vineyard.'*
>
> *"That evening he told the foreman to call the workers in and pay them, beginning with the last workers first. When those hired at five o'clock were paid, each received a full day's wage. When those hired first came to get their pay, they assumed they would receive more. But they, too, were paid a day's wage. When they received their pay, they protested to the owner, 'Those people worked only one hour, and yet you've paid them just as much as you paid us who worked all day in the scorching heat.'*
>
> *"He answered one of them, 'Friend, I haven't been unfair! Didn't you agree to work all day for the usual wage? Take your money and go. I wanted to pay this last worker the*

same as you. Is it against the law for me to do what I want with my money? Should you be jealous because I am kind to others?'

"So those who are last now will be first then, and those who are first will be last" (Matthew 20:1-16 NLT).

The message of Jesus seems crazy backward to those who hear it—he erases the old lines and redraws them in ways that include the excluded and embrace the undeserving. By doing so, his message becomes offensive not because of who gets left out but more so because of who gets let in. Much of Israel is left out, but Gentiles get let in? Prostitutes, sinners, and the worst tax collectors are at the front of the line, while keepers of the "law" are in the back of the line—if even in the line at all? No wonder people accused Jesus of being insane; this isn't the type of message they expected from the Messiah, and it certainly isn't the message we're used to hearing today.

Often we experience a Christianity that grows very uncomfortable with the inclusive lines that Jesus has drawn. In an effort to make ourselves feel a little better, we step into Jesus' sandals and pour as much water on those lines as needed, until they slowly begin to blur and fade away. Once they're gone, we redraw them in such a way that we become in, *but they become out.* But such exclusiveness is not the message of Jesus, no matter which way we try to redraw these lines.

Jesus includes the excluded, and he calls on his followers to be just like him.

In Jesus we find an inclusive rabbi who pushed back against conservative religious culture. Jesus made friends with those on the margins, though it was unpopular. He invited women to become his disciples, even though it was practically unheard of. He spoke up for the outcast who had no voice, and went toe to toe with the religious elite who thought they had God figured all out. The inclusive message of Jesus was countercultural and radically offensive in his culture—and it is in ours as well.

Instead of concentrating on how we can include the "other," too often in American Christianity the focus becomes on when, how, and finding the right justifications for excluding the "other." When I truly begin to appreciate the inclusive nature of Jesus, my heart laments at all the exclusiveness I see and experience.

I think of my female friends; women of wisdom, peace, discernment, and character who should be emulated by the rest of us. When I listen and learn from these women, I realize what an amazing leaders they would be in church—but many never will be leaders in that way because they are lacking one thing: male genitals. Wise and godly women have been excluded, not because of a lack of gifting, education, or ability, but because they were born with the wrong private parts.

I also think of a man who attended my former church who has an intellectual disability. He was friendly, faithful, and could always be counted on for a good laugh because he had absolutely no filter—yelling out at least six times during each sermon. One time in church my daughter quietly leaned over to tell me she had to go to the bathroom—and, in true form so that everyone heard, he shouted out, *"Hey! Pipe it down back there!"* It was hilarious. However, our friend has been asked to leave several churches because of his "disruptiveness." Instead of being loved and embraced for who he is, he has been repeatedly excluded from the people of God because of a disability.

We find plenty of other reasons to exclude people. We exclude because people have been divorced, exclude them for not signing on to our 18-page statements of faith, exclude them because of their mode of baptism, exclude them because of their sexual orientation, exclude them for rejecting predestination...we have become a religious culture focused on exclusion of the "other," instead of following the example of Jesus that focuses on finding ways for the radical *inclusion* of the "other."

Every day I drive by churches that proudly have "All Are Welcome" plastered across their signs; however, I rarely believe it—and I don't think others believe it either. Far too often, instead of church being something that exists for the "other," church becomes something that exists for the "like us" and the "willing to become like us."

And so, Christianity in America is dying.

But what if we rediscovered an undiluted inclusion and just started inclusively loving people the way Jesus did? What if we focused on removing barriers between each other and finding ways to include the "other" at the table beside us? What if we actually humbled ourselves and considered that the people we think are "out," might actually be on God's guest list? What if we actually included the excluded and showed radical, unconditional love toward the outcast?

When Jesus did this, it seems that people couldn't get enough of him. But Christians in America? I think most folks have had their fill of us. Call me crazy, but I think if we were to adopt a radical inclusiveness of the "other" like Jesus did, I think folks would flock to Jesus instead of run from him.

Our diluted understanding of Jesus has caused us to get our priorities backward. We must become people who remove barriers to God, instead of people who are busy installing new ones.

Yes, Jesus began his ministry with a radical message of inclusion—but he ended his ministry this way as well. In one of the final acts of Jesus, we find him tearing through the temple yards, kicking over tables, chasing out the animals, and sending the moneychangers away. This is a story many of us have heard from our youth, but we often miss that this is actually a story of *inclusion*.

In the temple, there was an area called the "Court of the Gentiles." This was the area where non-Jews could still come to the temple and find a safe place to experience God. However, this designated space in the temple—designated for the "other"—had slowly become a place of commerce, instead of a place where the "other" could encounter God. With all of the hustle and bustle of animals and moneychangers, it would have been impossible for an outsider to enter and experience God in any sort of meaningful way.

Like us, the religious people of Jesus' day had erected barriers between people and God, instead of tearing them down.

When we see Jesus chasing out the moneychangers and herding the animals, what we're actually seeing is Jesus recreating a safe place for the "other" to encounter God. With each animal He sends out, we see an image of the God who insists that holy space always be a safe place not just for the "like us" but for the "unlike us" as well. With each table he flips over, we see God himself making more room for outsiders to come in and have a place to find God. Jesus, then, becomes the one who focuses not on excluding—but undiluted inclusion.

The first time Jesus took a stand on including the outsiders, they tried to throw him off a cliff. The second time Jesus took a public stand for outsiders, they nailed him to a tree.

The message of Jesus is radically different from what we often experience in American Christianity. Over the past years, the inclusive Jesus has been watered-down and diluted to the point where he brings good news for "us," but not so much the "other." This watering down has distorted him to the point that we have, too many times, become the religious elite of Jesus' day, insisting that we would do a better job at drawing the lines between who is "in" and who is "out."

But this isn't the Jesus we find in scripture. In Jesus, we see an image of the God who insists on radical inclusion of others—even when we think they don't belong or deserve to be considered in.

As I continued to make my way through seminary and continued to grow as a person within my undiluted communities, I looked around and saw that I was surrounded by a lot of "others" whom I had previously excluded in my own mind because I had decided to draw the lines for God. There were a lot of people I had considered to be out, but now had come to realize they were so very clearly, in.

Like the religious elite of Jesus' time, we are destined for a life of being barrier makers and line drawers if we insist on holding on to a culturally diluted version of Jesus. However, when we rediscover the radical message of Jesus—a message that consistently, from beginning to end pronounced inclusion for the excluded, and love for the outcast—we rediscover a divine invitation to become the people who flip the tables, erase the lines, and remove barriers.

We are invited to join Jesus in practicing undiluted inclusion of the "other."

Let's stop being the religious elites who focus on when and how to keep people out, and instead endeavor to be the loving, inclusive followers of Jesus who unrelentingly invite the outsider to come in.

Those people we see who are busy drawing hard lines in the sand, busy banishing people from community because they don't fit the mold, and busy doing things that simply create more barriers that make it more difficult for outsiders to connect to God and each other? That's not what the undiluted Jesus looks like.

Jesus looks totally different.

If we want to be a people who live the undiluted, radical message of Jesus, we must become willing to experience undiluted change in our own lives that leads us to include the excluded, embrace the outcast, and lift up the marginalized.

CHAPTER 5

Undiluted Change

Where are your accusers? (JOHN 8:10 NLT)

Once I began to realize that the lines between who was in and who was out were far more generously drawn than I had previously thought, I felt the way I looked at others—and myself—begin to shift in my being. Prior to realizing that the others in seminary might equally be faithful Jesus followers—the Anglican heretics who might as well be Roman Catholic, the folks from the Assembly of God who believed in that demonic tongue-speaking stuff, the annoy-me-to-no-end reformed folks, the few social justice liberals I had met in the cafeteria, and the females who had no business taking a class on preaching, my heart was complexly focused on the "other," but for all the wrong reasons.

For the first several months, I'd come home from a rigorous day of classes and spend my evening complaining about the "others" who had it all wrong. My wife, Tracy, would get home from work around dinner time, and would grab a glass of wine and hop in the shower while I'd sit on the edge of the tub and unload about all the buttons that had been pushed in me that day.

"You'll never guess what this jackass said when I asked him why he was a Calvinist," I ranted. "He actually answered me with, 'Because it's on every page of scripture!'"

"And, can you believe that the second professor in my preaching class is a WOMAN? What kind of watered-down, liberal agenda nonsense is this?"

"Oh—and get this, the professor in my Spiritual Formation class said that one time he fell to the ground and felt like God was asking him to pray a prayer in gibberish!" Which was usually followed by what had been my favorite way of mocking people who speak in tongues—saying, "I bought a Hyundai but should have bought a Honda" eight times really fast (which always earned a stern look from my wife, who never found that funny).

"…And you won't believe what kind of book Zack has on his carrel in the library! It's an entire book about why the rapture is a man-made, false doctrine. What's worse, this book was written by one of the professors at THIS school! These people are C-R-A-Z-Y!"

Each night we went through this same routine, which rarely left an opportunity for her to get a word in edgewise. She often told people that she felt like she had gone to seminary too, because she heard about every little thing that had challenged the way I understood God and others. For the first few months, I was a miserable individual and wasted all of my energy focusing on how I was right, and the others were completely wrong. However, once I started to actually get to know people on a personal, relational level, I started to realize that these people—those who thought differently—were actually really great people. And what's more than that, I began to see that all of these "others" were actually authentically following Jesus, even if their expressions of faith and doctrine looked different from anything I had previously considered.

I slowly began to realize that I had been wasting my time with a hyper-focus on why all the "others" were doing it wrong and began to release the icy grip I had on everything I thought I knew. I finally accepted that I would be much happier if I just focused on myself and taking my own faith journey seriously and stopped worrying so much about everyone else. As soon as I gave up on the idea of changing everyone else and exchanged it for a commitment to change myself, I saw my heart begin to change.

I had come to realize that my version of the historic, Christian faith had been diluted to the point that it existed to change others instead of something designed to first change me. It is strange how so often the "others" get left out, except when we look at the part of the gospel designed to confront broken thinking and change people. When we get to *that* part, surely it's there for someone else. To me, the message of Jesus had become something that was designed to fix everything that was broken in *them,* and I had missed the entire fact that it was first supposed to be fixing something that was desperately broken inside *me.*

You see, when we view the radical message of Jesus as something designed to change the "other" before we allow it to first and primarily radically change our own selves, we end up living a diluted faith that is absent its full potency. In fact, such a backward faith structure becomes functionally worthless; and worse, the expressions of this distorted version of Jesus becomes offensive to those around us—pushing us and those we encounter deeper into brokenness instead of in the direction of restoration and wholeness.

The radical message of Jesus is not supposed to be this way.

Yes—the radical message is good news for the "other" and the church is called to inclusively exist for the "other," but the transformational aspect of Jesus' message starts right here—with you and me. Until we let that happen? Well, until we allow it to radically change and soften our own hearts, we've got no business doing anything other than loving and including others.

For far too long in much of American Christian Culture, our movement has been defined not by Jesus—but by who we think our "common enemy" is. First they told us the enemy was the people who wanted to teach evolution in our schools. Then they told us it was the people who wanted to stop teacher-led prayer in schools. Moving into the 1980s, we were told that the enemy was the liberal agenda, and the existence of legalized abortion. Most recently, Christian culture has tried to convince us that our new enemy is the "gay agenda" and the legalization of same-sex marriage.

For too long, we've seen the gospel as something that exists to change whoever we define as our common enemy.

For some reason war is never the enemy. Cyclical poverty is never the enemy. A system that jails black men at shockingly disproportionate rates than whites is never the enemy. Corporate wealth and greed is never the enemy. Run-away defense spending is never the enemy…

And certainly, we are never the enemy.

But what if we are?

What if we are actually the most destructive enemy of all, and that we're sidetracking the Kingdom of God when we focus on fighting people instead of reforming ourselves? What if our own arrogance, greed, self-centeredness, and self-righteousness is actually the enemy who is harming the future of the Jesus movement most?

I think it is.

I think we are.

Every time I see a confrontational Christian bumper sticker on a car in the church parking lot, I'm reminded that once again we have misidentified the real enemy. We have been our own worst enemy all along, because we've diluted the message of Jesus down to something designed to change the others, without first radically changing ourselves.

In the life of Jesus, we see him encounter a religious culture that had a very similar problem as ours. While the religious conservatives weren't typically inclusive of the "other," they certainly did focus on the "other" a good portion of the time—and for all the wrong reasons. They too, had a faith that was distorted into something that needed to be applied to the other, and change the other without actually changing themselves.

This idea of changing the others without first changing ourselves, is being a hypocrite.

One of my favorite stories of Jesus is when he is presented with a woman whom the religious leaders had accused of committing a capital offense, and wished to execute. While we don't know the entire backstory—different scholars have different takes on what may or may not have led up to this encounter—we do know that Jesus was given the opportunity to approve an execution that the law said was just. It was the ultimate opportunity to pass judgment.

As Jesus surveyed the situation, he saw on one side, religious conservatives who *thought* they had all their crap in one bag, and on the other, a woman who had committed adultery and deserved to be stoned to death. By human eyes, the enemy to cultural morality and good order seemed clear—surely, it was the woman who didn't keep her sexual behavior in line with the cultural norms or the law. Setting an example of her would have been seemingly "good" for the overall community.

But that's not how the story plays out.

From John chapter 8, we find the story in its entirety:

> *Jesus returned to the Mount of Olives, but early the next morning he was back again at the Temple. A crowd soon gathered, and he sat down and taught them. As he was speaking, the teachers of religious law and the Pharisees brought a woman who had been caught in the act of adultery. They put her in front of the crowd.*
>
> *"Teacher," they said to Jesus, "this woman was caught in the act of adultery. The law of Moses says to stone her. What do you say?"*
>
> *They were trying to trap him into saying something they could use against him, but Jesus stooped down and wrote in the dust with his finger. They kept demanding an answer, so he stood up again and said, "All right, but let the one who has never sinned throw the first stone!" Then he stooped down again and wrote in the dust.*

When the accusers heard this, they slipped away one by one, beginning with the oldest, until only Jesus was left in the middle of the crowd with the woman. Then Jesus stood up again and said to the woman, "Where are your accusers? Didn't even one of them condemn you?"

"No, Lord," she said.

And Jesus said, "Neither do I. Go and sin no more" (John 8:1-11 NLT).

Given an opportunity to agree upon a common enemy and given the opportunity to express indignation over the sins and cultural destructiveness of the "other," Jesus instead turns the tables on the religious elite and reminds them that they would be much better off to worry about their own behavior. Their sins are serious enough, Jesus reminds them, that they probably should be so focused on correcting their individual issues that they aren't left with any time to walk around expressing indignation over the perceived sins of others.

It is as if Jesus said, "Let you worry about you, and let her worry about her."

The apostle Paul expresses a very similar sentiment—and actually does so in much stronger terms when he says:

This is a trustworthy saying, and everyone should accept it: "Christ Jesus came into the world to save sinners"—and I am the worst of them all. But God had mercy on me so that Christ Jesus could use me as a prime example of his great patience with even the worst sinners. Then others will realize that they, too, can believe in him and receive eternal life (1 Timothy 1:15-16 NLT).

What Paul argues here is countercultural to what we often experience, which too frequently seems to see a need to be fighting an external, common enemy. When our perceived enemy doesn't actually turn out to be an enemy, we simply replace it with a new person, group or issue and press on with the same paradigm structure. However, instead of encouraging us to wage the next conservative culture war, Paul actually says that the key to changing the hearts of others is through a radical humility that acknowledges our shortcomings and sins to be actually *worse* than theirs.

That's right—we are actually *worse* than whoever we think "they" are.

Worse than that Supreme Court Justice who keeps voting to uphold Row vs. Wade.

Worse than that female Universalist minister down the street who marries same-sex couples every Sunday afternoon.

Worse than Nancy Pelosi.

Worse than those "lazy" people on food stamps who are "sucking the nation dry."

Worse than those "illegal immigrants".

Worse than that blogger who you *think* is a heretic.

Just replace "they" with whoever it is you *think* is the enemy—and know this: you should consider yourself to be a worse sinner than how you perceive them to be.

But do we actually believe that? Do we believe that only the sinless should throw the stones and that we are the worst of sinners who serve as examples that God is patient with people who test his patience?

Do we really believe that we should be exhausting ourselves reforming our own hearts, long before we ever dream of trying to reform what's wrong in the hearts of others?

I'm not sure that we do.

If we did, I think we'd have a lot fewer confrontational Christian bumper stickers in the church parking lot.

Until we are willing to let go of a hyper-focus on changing others and exchange it for a humble desire to focus inward, this broken thinking has the potential to assimilate into all areas of our worldview. Once that happens, we end up with a distorted way of seeing others—one that tends to see everyone else as needing to change, and misses the fact that Jesus wants to change *us*.

This beam in our eye? It distorts our vision to the point where we are completely unable to see our brother's speck for what it actually is. However, if we take the time to adequately remove this beam that's blocking our vision, we might even discover that what we *thought* was a speck in our brother's eye wasn't actually a speck at all—but a speck in our own which simply got projected onto him.

The message of Jesus was never intended to be diluted and simmered down into something that exists to change the other without first radically changing ourselves. However, once we are able to humbly accept that for many of us Christian culture has passed us down an Americanized Christianity that does exactly that, we are able to finally begin to break free and experience the true, intoxicating nature of the message of Jesus.

A message that will radically change *us* if we will let it.

Once I came to fully embrace that I too had been living a diluted Christianity that focused on what needed to change in the "others" instead of what needed to change in me, my evening discussions with Tracy changed in their tone and content. Instead of coming home pissed off about what some Mark Driscoll wannabe said in class, I came home wrestling with actual concepts about God—interested in how it might first change me, instead of how it might be applied to others. Certainly, I still talked about the many buttons that had been pushed that day (usually by Mark Driscoll wannabes), but once I stopped seeing the "others" as the ones who had God all misunderstood, the kind of buttons pushed inside me changed. Now, it was my own buttons—my own shortcomings, my own misunderstandings about who God is and how he relates to us—that capitalized my time and emotional attention.

I was used to having stones in my hands, but I realized now I needed both hands free to get to work...

On me.

American religious culture invites us to embrace a life in the "Lord's Army," as together we fight to change or destroy subtle enemies of the faith. For those of us who have grown up in this cultural framework, it has taught us to see ourselves as being correct and everything and everyone else, needing to change. This arrogant (dare I say sinful) attitude has made the beautiful message of Jesus anything but appealing—directly rubbing against the biblical instruction to "make the gospel attractive" (Titus 2:9-12). Living this kind of life is exhausting, and given enough time, turns us into angry culture warriors intent on "taking America back," shutting out voices we disagree with, and making more enemies than friends.

Given enough time, we might actually have well-defined arm muscles from all the rocks we're throwing, but realize our own heart muscles have atrophied from lack of use.

This isn't what Jesus had in mind.

When we rediscover the radical message of Jesus, we realize that we've been given an invitation to experience undiluted change in our own lives.

His is an invitation to look down at our dusty shoes, to drop our stones in the dirt beside us, and go back home until we ourselves have been radically transformed to such a degree that we become walking examples of God's love and patience. If we do that, we just might achieve the change we desire in others, not by throwing stones, but from directing our demand for change inward.

CHAPTER 6

Undiluted Tension

*"I do believe, help me overcome
my unbelief!"* (MARK 9:24)

Learning to love others while focusing on how the message of Jesus might first and foremost change me freed me to begin a new faith journey. It was an exciting journey, but quickly became a journey filled with the tension that wrestling with one's faith often brings. Growing up in conservative evangelicalism and then getting caught up into fundamentalism during my teen years, I was never introduced to any level of tension in my faith—only black and whiteness. Though I had never realized it, black and whiteness was the water, and I was the fish who had no idea what he was swimming in—but kept swimming I did, as there was something comfortable about that way of living out my faith.

Almost all questions had cut-and-dried answers, truth was absolute and completely accessible for anyone who wanted to know it, and every verse in the Bible had a clear and obvious interpretation. I don't remember there ever being any mystery to God, or even any hard questions that didn't have good answers, other than the question of: "Why does God choose some people to go to heaven, and choose other people to go to hell?" Even then I was given a cut-and-dried answer that took no thought to formulate: "Just because you enjoy adopting children doesn't mean you can adopt them all."

Mine wasn't a faith of mystery, tension, or confidence with doubt, but was a faith that thought it had the mysteries of God completely figured out. On one hand, there was no fun in a Christian faith that had answers for everything—but it was safe and comfortable, at least.

And so, for far too long I held on to it—fiercely.

Some say that part of our nature is a craving for boundaries and clear answers as a way of creating safety. Parenting books will tell you that children actually crave rules and structure, and that when this structure is consistently maintained, it creates a sense of safety and predictability for them. As adults, I think many of us tend to gravitate toward this inner craving when it comes to spirituality—or, at least I did. Getting lost into black-and-white Christian religion was an easy choice for me, not because it was necessarily true, but because it was clear-cut and predictable. In this paradigm of faith, I didn't need to worry about the questions and just needed to stay busy memorizing the answers. This roadmap to faith was comfortable, safe, and required very little thinking on my part, which is what made it so painful to let go of.

As I slowly tumbled down the deeper and deeper rabbit hole that became seminary, I was soon faced with my biggest fear: I didn't know that much about God, about the Bible, or anything else, really. I had assumed that going to seminary would simply reinforce everything I already knew, and reinforce the paradigm I arrived with. Seminary, I had hoped, would just be Liberty University on steroids; I had budgeted for God, Jesus, the Bible, and everything else to become more and more black and white, safer, and more comfortable. The deeper I went, however, everything became a whole lot grayer, more obscure, and less absolute. Before I had realized it, I found myself entering into undiluted tension.

It was frightening at first.

As I grew to understand the Bible better and grew to have a greater understanding of the culture Jesus lived in, I came to the realization that my previous faith structure had become diluted with the last thing that one would think could dilute faith: answers. The nonexistence of questions without answers, the clear-cut nature of understanding the intended

meaning of scripture, the lack of mystery with God—it diluted (and ultimately distorted) my faith, instead of inviting me into the tension of faith,
where I believe Jesus wants to invite us.

When we rediscover the radical nature of the message of Jesus, we find
an embrace of tension instead of the idolatry of certainty that so many of
us have grown accustom to. When Jesus rolls up on the scene, we find the
dominant cultural discussion among people of faith to be quite similar to
what we find today. With so many laws in the Hebrew Scriptures (613 to
be exact), the religious leaders of Jesus' day spent much of their time debating what it meant to keep each one.

Since rules often are less than cut and dried (especially if there are no
footnotes to give one guidance in circumstances that don't seem to fit the
mold), these 613 laws provided generations worth of debate fodder. For
example, while the prohibition of working on the Sabbath may seem cut
and dried, religious leaders spent countless time trying to figure out what
that law actually meant—as they would with so many others.

Did it mean they couldn't harvest grain to eat on the Sabbath?

Did it mean they couldn't help someone in need if they encountered
the person on the Sabbath?

Did it mean they couldn't tend to a sick animal if the sickness or injury
happened to fall on the Sabbath?

The religious leaders had plenty of questions about the law to
haunt them.

Like us, the religious leaders of the day (and those who came before
them) weren't major fans of tension and uncertainly. To relieve some of
the tension created by unanswered questions in the law, an oral version of
the Torah had been developed, which gave people interpretive guidance
on how to properly understand and apply the law to their lives. Many
believed that the law contained clandestine interpretations that needed to
be drawn out, so oral traditions of interpretation became the tool used to
relieve the tension of unanswered questions. Ironically, this in some ways
actually created *more* tension in the culture because different rabbis had

vastly different interpretations of what the law actually meant—and thus the endless cycle of theological debating ensued.

Not at all unlike the culture we find ourselves in today.

Jesus often weighed in on these debates, but not in the way one might have expected Messiah to do. Instead of giving black and white clarity to the law, we often find Jesus answering a question with another question, speaking to the attitude or motivation behind the question. And at other times we find him not just refusing to clarify the law, but instead find him disagreeing with it and ordering that the law itself no longer be followed—such as in the case of retributive violence.

In some ways when Jesus answered questions, he seems on the surface more like a politician dancing around the question rather than the only one who could possibly clarify the teachings of the law. This wasn't exactly what the religious teachers were looking to hear—they craved a type of black and whiteness that could be applied in cookie-cutter format—not a faith that invites one into tension and uncertainty.

Unanswered questions make us uncomfortable, but instead of embracing the tension of uncertainty, we opt to find ways to fill in the blanks and relieve ourselves of the tension. We create our own oral law too—not because more black and whiteness is necessarily true, but because black and whiteness is easier than living in a sea of gray.

And so we dilute the message of Jesus when we try to tell people—or even ourselves—that a life following the way of Jesus is all plain and simple.

It's not. The message of Jesus is actually quite complex, and often will create more tension than it relieves.

Scripture reveals to us that during the ministry of Jesus, he preferred to teach by way of parable. As we sift through the life of Jesus, it's hard to flip too many pages without seeing him tell some sort of riddle-laden story. In fact, in Mark's Gospel we actually find a verse that says there were times when Jesus insisted on using parables, and nothing but parables:

> *In fact, in his public ministry he never taught without using parables...* (Mark 4:34 NLT).

Growing up, the parables of Jesus confused the daylights out of me. Reading the parables of Jesus was like looking at a math word problem—I wasn't sure what the meaning of X was. When I asked the Sunday school teacher why Jesus spoke in parables all the time, I was simply told, "Jesus taught in parables because it was an easy way to explain things so that people would understand."

I found the answer less than compelling, even at eight.

What's so clear and simple about a lady sweeping her house to find a nickel?

And that future telling via a fig tree? Not so clear on that one either.

Foolish virgins who forgot to recharge the batteries to their flashlights?

Yeah—not so straight and forward if you ask me. Too many of us have been taught, and come to believe, that the teachings of Jesus—especially parables—are actually easy to understand, when in fact, they are not. Oftentimes the stories Jesus tells provoke infinitely more questions than they do answers. Like the religious leaders of Jesus' time, this creates a significant amount of discomfort for us, and we resist the tension in favor of our own, man-made, black and whiteness.

Jesus didn't intend much of his teaching to be always clear, black and white, or even easily understandable—he intended much of it to be complex, obscure on the surface, and something that invites us into undiluted tension instead of an idolatry that becomes our own certainty. In Matthew's Gospel, Jesus actually tells his disciples that he taught in parables in order to make his teachings more obscure, and actually for the purpose of confusing the religious elite. This constant teaching by way of parable didn't have anything to do with making things easier to understand or making truth accessible, but instead was designed to create tension and force hearers to actually enter into that tension and wrestle with the message in order to discover the underlying truth.

Jesus never wanted us to have canned, prefabricated answers for every issue—he wants us to wrestle with the complexity of his message over and over again, until we are able to hold truth in tandem with tension. Truth must be held humbly next to the same hand that holds our doubt.

Jesus, I believe, wants us to embrace the tension of faith and repent of our own need for certainty.

In Mark chapter 9, we discover one of my favorite all-time stories in the Bible. The story is of a man who approached Jesus, and asked Jesus to heal his son. The disciples of Jesus had tried, unsuccessfully, and so the man turns to Jesus as his last stop to find healing for his son:

> *"A man in the crowd answered, "Teacher, I brought you my son, who is possessed by a spirit that has robbed him of speech. Whenever it seizes him, it throws him to the ground. He foams at the mouth, gnashes his teeth and becomes rigid. I asked your disciples to drive out the spirit, but they could not."*
>
> *"You unbelieving generation," Jesus replied, "how long shall I stay with you? How long shall I put up with you? Bring the boy to me."*
>
> *So they brought him. When the spirit saw Jesus, it immediately threw the boy into a convulsion. He fell to the ground and rolled around, foaming at the mouth.*
>
> *Jesus asked the boy's father, "How long has he been like this?"*
>
> *"From childhood," he answered. "It has often thrown him into fire or water to kill him. But if you can do anything, take pity on us and help us."*
>
> *"'If you can'?" said Jesus. "Everything is possible for him who believes."*
>
> *Immediately the boy's father exclaimed, "I do believe; help me overcome my unbelief!"* (Mark 9:17-24)

What I love most about this story is the illustration of holding our belief and our unbelief in tension with one another, and that this tension actually invites us to live relationally with God. The man in the story tells Jesus, "I believe; help me overcome my unbelief!" in a beautiful example of what it means to wrestle in the tension of faith—believing, but still needing help in our unbelief. Understanding, but still needing help to understand. In the story, Jesus in fact does help the man—and heals his son. Admitting his need for help in unbelief led to an opportunity to experience God in a deeper and more meaningful way; it led to a profound encounter with Jesus. Of all the people I meet in scripture, I find this man perhaps the most authentic of all, because he readily admitted holding belief and unbelief, knowledge and lack of understanding, all in tension—openly, and honestly.

You and I can experience God in deeper and more undiluted ways too, when we let go of our need for certainty and simply embrace the tension that Jesus invites us into. A faith that has it all figured out? That's a diluted version. But when we jump into the tension of Christian faith, one that invites us to follow Jesus while still being open and honest about our doubts, we discover a deeper reliance on God.

What is often missed in this scripture story is that when the man was able to openly and authentically be real about the tension of faith and doubt, it allowed him to have a *relational* encounter with Jesus that actually *strengthened* his faith. When he asks, "help me overcome my unbelief," he opens the door to begin experiencing God at work in his life, and opens the door to a relationship that can bring peace and hope amid tension and doubt. What I really find encouraging about this story is that while it occurs directly after Jesus chided people for their unbelief, Jesus readily embraces the one person in the crowd who was simply open and authentic in expressing faith and doubt in tension with one another. Jesus, we see, responds favorably to those who are real and authentic regarding their doubts.

I think Jesus designed his teaching to be less than clear for a reason. As we saw in Chapter 2, Jesus claims that all scripture points to him. The more we see the relational side of God through the person and work of Jesus, the more obvious it becomes that Jesus wanted us to have a healthy, relational dependency, in community with him. Had his teachings all been black and white, had they simply been condensed into a no-room-for-debate document designed to give us all of the clear-cut answers we long for, our hope and dependency would be on the answers themselves, instead of the person who can give them.

And, that's not what we were designed for.

I think Jesus leaves us in the questions so that we'll be motivated to keep following him.

While we may crave answers for everything, we don't actually need them—nor does God want us to have them. If we did, those answers just might themselves become our God and our source of comfort. Instead, Jesus invites us to embrace belief and unbelief, certainty and doubt, understanding and confusion, all in the same tension.

Embracing the tension of our faith represents the beginning stage of entering into the "Kingdom of Heaven" that Jesus so often spoke about. Jesus, the rabbi who loved to include children in his ministry, once used children as an illustration to those who were considering following him. Pointing out the children in their midst, Jesus told them that unless they were willing to become like children all over again, they would never enter into the Kingdom that is readily available for all to enter. Unfortunately, this story often gets misused—I remember as a child having this explained to me as meaning that in order to enter the Kingdom, I needed to blindly and faithfully believe whatever was taught to me. However, instead of a principle intended to dominate and control other people, what Jesus was saying was quite different: in this story Jesus teaches us that if we want to fully experience God, we need to set aside our certainty and become willing to no longer insist that we have all the answers.

Like a child.

Children don't have all the answers, but they do have lots of questions—and asking those questions leads to learning, and often relearning, everything they know. If you and I want to experience the radical message of Jesus in a new way, we need to become willing to set aside what we *think* we know, and be content to sit with questions and uncertainty as we begin a process of relearning and rediscovery.

Becoming like a child—letting go of my certainty in exchange for questions and tension—saved my faith.

As months turned to a year at Gordon-Conwell, and a year turned into two, I realized how little I was certain of anything anymore. I encountered skilled theologians who equally loved Jesus but disagreed strongly on theology, Greek words that had flavor and nuance lost in the English translations of scripture, and far more room for "educated guesses" than I had ever dreamed existed in theology. As I let go of my idol of certainty and exchanged it for life in the tension between belief and doubt, knowledge and misunderstanding, I found myself in a deeper relational reliance on God than I had ever experienced before. In time, I realized that my hope, trust, and previous faith had all been rooted in the securities of my answers, instead of the security of Jesus. In the undiluted tension however, I found myself working diligently to understand God—yet learning to ask him to help me overcome my unbelief.

In time, I discovered that I no longer needed answers for everything, and exchanged answers for actual faith, trust—and even doubt—in Jesus.

And so can you.

If we want to rediscover the radical message of Jesus, we need to stop diluting it by letting ourselves believe that this is something cut and dried, and stop forcing ourselves to seek truth only in the black and whiteness. Instead, we need to embrace the fact that the message of Jesus is at times simple, at other times obscure, frequently mysterious, and is something that often creates more questions than answers.

Once we let go of our idolatry of certainty and embrace living in the tension, we find that we rediscover a faith that actually relies on Jesus.

Which, I believe, is exactly where he wants us.

Holding in tension both belief and unbelief.

Certainty and doubt.

Clarity and confusion.

Together, in tension.

The radical message of Jesus is that we can be real and authentic about our faith and doubts, and that doing so might actually be the path to most fully experiencing him.

Once we let go and finally embrace that the Christian life was one intended to be lived in tension, we'll find that we actually grow to trust and experience God in deeper and more relational ways. Instead of trusting in our answers, we'll find that we're forced to begin placing our trust in him. Instead of relaxing in the security of our knowledge, we are forced to find peace simply in following him the best we are able. As a result of this trust and doubt, faith and uncertainty, we end up developing a healthy intimacy and level of trust in the God who invited us into the tension in the first place.

We discover who we were made to be—people who depend on God in a real, intimate, and relational way.

But to get there, we've got to learn how to say, "I believe, help me overcome my unbelief."

CHAPTER 7

Undiluted Difficulty

...the Son of Man has no place to lay
his head (MATTHEW 8:20).

Ironically, when we dilute the radical message of Jesus into something that is clear-cut and black and white, we actually create a faith that is in many ways, easier. Ridged religion might be burdensome, but it is actually quite easy—you simply memorize the list of things you don't do, surround yourself with like-minded people, and learn to settle into the program. Once you assimilate, keeping up becomes less and less difficult. However, as I began to more fully reorient on Jesus, living in the community, learned to be inclusive of others while focusing on changing myself, and more fully learned to live in the tension, I began to discover that actually following Jesus doesn't get progressively easier.

Strangely enough, following the radical message of Jesus is quite hard. Being a Christian can be easy, but a Jesus follower...not so much.

In my lifetime I've experienced enough altar calls at church services, teen events, and Christian campfire services to have the American selling points on following Jesus memorized. So ingrained they were on my memory, that even when I started preaching as an adult, the same old misrepresentations of my youth naturally flowed from my lips, impacting yet another generation with bad PR on what it means to follow Jesus. Usually, these services went something like this: an aggressive message on why going to hell would be like putting your face in the fire while listening to AC/DC, and that the solution to hell is to "ask Jesus into your heart." In this paradigm, Jesus becomes the ticket out of a bad situation, and all that's required to get your free pass is to "repeat this simple prayer after me."

And, poof...you're "saved" and now a fully vetted Jesus follower.

American Christianity has been poorly marketing Jesus in this way for years. The deep, mysterious, and beautifully difficult message of Jesus becomes diluted to the point that we sing, "I have decided to follow Jesus" or "All to Jesus I Surrender" as we make our way up the aisle—thinking that following Jesus is actually that simple. What's worse is that often our motivation for "asking Jesus into our hearts" is that we're petrified of the myriad of ways that Jesus will have us tortured for eternity if we don't properly pray the "sinner's prayer" to show him that we love him back. From that night forward, we're supposed to faithfully attend a "Bible-be-lieving church" and destroy our Guns n' Roses CDs in order to show that we actually meant it when we prayed it.

In American Christianity, we're often sold this bill of goods that makes following Jesus look relatively easy...as if it were a singular event instead of a radical new lifestyle.

Said the magic prayer? Check.

Willing to go to church? Check.

Going to work really hard to cut back on how much I use the "F word"? Check.

The rewards of following this simple, relatively easy checklist of what it means to follow Jesus supposedly has a huge payout. Not only do we get to claim our "get out of hell free" card, but we also get to claim a host of promises designed to make life better: God-ordained "prosperity," God's "hedge of protection," and the fact that God now has a "wonderful plan for our life" that he will be "faithful to complete." Following Jesus, we are led to believe, is a relatively easy decision to make and live out—and as a result, will help us achieve the American dream in our own lives.

This sounds great, if it were actually true.

But, it's not.

This diluted marketing of what it looks like to actually follow Jesus is killing us. As a result, we now live in a country where the vast majority identify themselves as Christians, yet very few of them seem to have much resemblance to the Jesus I read about in scripture—myself included. What was once an invitation to actually follow and learn to become like Jesus, has been diluted into something that can be taken care of in a single prayer, in a single act, or in a single decision. The result of this diluted gospel is that we're led to believe, either directly or through omission, that following Jesus is the ticket to a better life by the world's standards.

Jesus, as it turns out, has a completely different standard for what a "better" life looks like.

One of my favorite movie lines of all time is from the movie *Armageddon*. With a colossal asteroid streaking toward earth, a band of misfit oil drillers mixed with legitimate astronauts head into space to intercept and destroy the asteroid, thus saving the future of humanity. Once their spacecraft reaches the asteroid, however, they are confronted by a scary, inhospitable world. As one of the spacecrafts prepares for what ends up being a crash landing, the character played by Owen Wilson screams out, "THIS ISN'T AS BAD AS I THOUGHT IT WOULD BE—IT'S WAY WORSE!"

When I think about what it means to actually follow Jesus—to learn to be like him and to attempt to live out the radical nature of his message—I often think back to that movie. Living like Jesus isn't a ticket to wealth, prosperity, or the American dream. When we dilute what it means to actually follow him, people end up like the guy on the asteroid when they finally realize, "This isn't as bad as I thought it would be—it's way worse."

If you're coming into this with American cultural understandings of a "better life," this is going to be way, way worse.

What's crazy, is that when we rediscover the radical message of Jesus, we find that he too warned people that following him might be way worse than what they envision. In Matthew chapter 8, we find a man who told Jesus that he would like to become a follower. Instead of saying, "Sure thing, just repeat this simple prayer after me," however, Jesus actually warns the man that making the decision to not just pay mental ascent to Jesus but actually follow him, could have devastating results by cultural standards. *"Foxes have holes and birds of the air have nests, but the Son of Man has no place to lay his head,"* Jesus warns him in Matthew 8:20.

Instead of affirming that becoming a follower was the ticket to a richer and fuller life, and instead of affirming that the decision to follow would be the ticket to living your "best life now," Jesus responds with a harsh dose of truth. It's as if Jesus is saying, "You wanna follow me? Great. But before you do, just know this, I'm a homeless guy. Most nights, I find a ditch to crash in for the evening…and if I'm lucky, someone gives me a little food. So if I'm homeless and have nowhere to go, and you're saying you'd like to follow me, just know that this will probably make you a homeless guy too."

This isn't the only time Jesus says stuff like this. In the very next verse, another person asks to follow Jesus but says he wants to first spend some time with his father who was likely in the last years of his life. Jesus' response wasn't, "Sure thing, handle your business," it was, "If you want to follow me, you're not going to have time for a lot of the stuff that right now seems important to you."

Not exactly the response the man was expecting.

Over and over again we find Jesus not telling people that following would be easy or lead to prosperity, but warning them that—at least from a practical standpoint—following could actually wreck their lives. At one point Jesus goes to some rather extreme examples, telling people that they actually needed to hate their lives, and then warning them that in order to follow, they need to be willing to first pick up a cross.

Pick up a cross?

Yeah, that was a pretty vile symbol in those days. It's as if Jesus is telling people, "If you want to follow me, you'd better start tying your noose now, because following me will likely get you killed." And, true to his word, all of his disciples, less John, found that to be more than simply a metaphor.

Jesus sells himself a wee bit different from the way he tends to be sold in American Christianity, no?

Endeavoring to live a life that actually looks like Jesus isn't a ticket to prosperity, but rather a ticket to guaranteed hardships. By the time I had given up on the Christian religion and simply started trying to live in a way that emulated the teachings of Jesus, I quickly began to realize how diluted American Christianity had become with this false notion that following Jesus is somehow a ticket to the "good life" by cultural standards—it's not. The undiluted version I slowly rediscovered, actually was something that invites us not into life as we expect, but invites us to experience a form of death.

Death to ourselves.

Death to our secret aspirations.

Death to what technically might be our "rights."

Death to hopes of having our best life, now.

Yes, the invitation of Jesus is an invitation to gain—but only by way of loss, first. Of all the religious leaders in history, the message of Jesus is the most bizarre, because instead of teaching us how to increase our life (as we understand it), the message of Jesus is an invitation to willingly walk into a million forms of death.

It is a crazy different type of message. The diluted, plastic American version of Jesus fits right into the American dream, set neatly on the mantle beside our other valuables. Instead of the message often sent by American Christianity however, the undiluted message of Jesus reminds us that we can experience the ultimate life if, and only if, we first become willing to lay that life down. And these aren't small losses Jesus is talking about. Jesus invites us to lose everything—including our very lives—as part of the journey that ultimately teaches us a new definition of what it means to truly experience an undiluted life.

When Tracy and I started seminary (I say Tracy and I, because our intense evening discussions about my day meant that she was essentially in seminary as well), we had both hoped to one day adopt a child. In fact, the evening we met for the first time at a wedding reception, our conversation quickly found its way into a joint passion to one day adopt—something that was a significant factor in our initial attraction to each other. Initially, we had discussed having biological children first (I really, really wanted a biological son for what I now see as having been foolish reasons) and that we would eventually fit an adoption into our master plan whenever it was the most convenient. Once my transformation began however, I quickly realized that Jesus wasn't interested in me doing what fit nicely into my life (*"let the dead bury the dead"*). He wasn't interested in us just being another good, evangelical household with an adopted child in tow. Jesus, I became convinced, was more interested in inviting me to lay down my own personal aspirations in order to embrace a life that favored the needs of others. In my case, it meant setting aside my desire for biological children in order to fully embrace adoption as a "lifestyle," and fully devote myself to providing a family to children who otherwise would have none.

Accepting Jesus' radical invitation to care for the poor, hungry, and naked quickly became obvious to us. Without even needing any discussion, we filled out the paperwork to grow our family by adopting two girls from Peru and decided that we would adopt older children whose risk of "aging out" of the orphanage and ending up in a life of exploitation, were high. After a long and expensive process, I found myself taking a semester off from seminary in order to travel to Peru to finalize the adoption and bring our girls home.

The day we met the girls was the most emotional day of my life. When we walked through the towering steel doors to enter into the dirt courtyard, I saw my girls for the very first time as they were waving to us from the other side of a large door with bars and a giant paddle lock, much like in a prison. Through my tears, I shouted to them, "Estamos aquí! Estamos aquí!" The afternoon was filled with lots of hugs, beaming faces, quickly learning how to use an iPod they found in my wife's purse, and talk of family.

It was all so perfect…until day four when we left the orphanage for the last time, and moved into temporary living quarters in Lima.

That's when the violence started.

As we watched our youngest quickly embrace the idea of family without any desire to look back, we watched our oldest daughter respond violently to being placed in a family. We quickly realized that regardless what people were telling us, the medical records we had been given could not possibly be accurate. During a month of pending legalities prior to the adoption being finalized in the Peruvian courts, our agency representative revisited the orphanage desperately seeking more information. Yet, all we were told is that "We've never seen anyone hurt before."

We quickly watched everything spiral out of control before our very eyes. Toward the end of the legal waiting period required to finalize the adoption, the social workers came by the hotel and gave us a serious heart-to-heart. They told us that our oldest did not want to complete the adoption, and that if she didn't agree to the adoption, they would send both her and her little sister to a new orphanage...never to have a chance at adoption again. A twelve-year-old girl was being given the opportunity to make a permanent life decision for her eight-year-old sister. Apart from her ability to choose for both herself and her sister, we were also being advised by the social workers that it would not be wise to complete the adoption. "If you try to raise this child, you'll end up divorced," they warned us. Yet, we both knew that sending *both* girls back to an orphanage, considering this was their one-shot-deal to ever have a family and avoid a life of predictable exploitation, wasn't an option on the table. We pressed forward as our oldest eventually consented to finalize the legalities, as we endured an almost daily plague of violent behavior. Eventually, enough became enough, and I had it out with God.

As I paced back and forth on the large open patio, a cup of Peruvian coffee in one hand and an American cigarette in the other, I let God know what was on my mind—without holding back.

"This one is on you, man. I came here because YOU told me to defend the fatherless. I came here because YOU told me to encourage the oppressed. I'm not here because I have fertility issues and need to be here—I'm here because I decided to live radically like Jesus. So this one is on YOU. The table is set, you have a chair, it's now your turn to show up for dinner."

After dropping a few f-bombs and an "in Jesus name, Amen," I made a decision to just keep walking forward, and to leave the rest up to God.

The day after the legalities were finalized in court, the orphanage finally handed over what we knew existed all along: hidden medical records that validated and confirmed everything we had been experiencing.

The next year and a half after we returned to the States was a depressing hell. We fought hard for my daughter, and dedicated our lives to "therapeutic parenting," a process that takes two people and about 36 hours in a day. While one daughter was flourishing and bonding to family, one was floundering and rejecting. Each day was filled with moments of joy on one hand, and moments of profound sadness the next. We went through four hospitalizations in seven months, and even more ER visits and 911 calls that didn't always result in hospitalization. When not hospitalized, our home was converted into a hospital-like state. Our days were filled with violence and threats of violence to the point that we had alarms on our bedroom doors to protect us from being assaulted in our sleep, a key lock on the knife drawer, had a large stock of plastic cups and plates, and completely gutted our house of anything glass, sharp, or that could be remotely used or converted into a weapon. We went to every length possible to keep everyone safe, and to give her every opportunity possible to live in a family setting safely.

When not driving to hospitals for visitations and therapy, or in hospital mode at home, we were meeting with clinical team members who focused on: family preservation in adoptions, attachment therapy every Wednesday, in-home intensive therapy 3-4 days a week, respite organizations, personal counselors (everybody needs one!), the chief of psychiatry from Tufts Medical Center, school clinicians (we secured a therapeutic school), DCF social workers (who we asked to come on the team voluntarily), and a host of others. We literally "maximized servicing" as our lives were consumed with giving our daughter the best possible chance to make it in a family unit. We barely even worked, allowing our finances to go down the toilet so that we could fully devote our lives to serving our daughter.

All this while I attempted to finish seminary.

Eventually the large team of providers made it clear to us that the situation simply wasn't safe to continue, and we had to pursue permanent, out-of-home placement for the safety of everyone in the family. It was the most devastating and difficult decision of our lives—something we had never fully imagined when we started the journey.

Living out the radical message of Jesus—especially in regard to caring for the "least of these" wasn't like anything I had been taught. Instead of a ticket to prosperity, it placed us on the fast track to hardship. Instead of an invitation to life, it became an invitation to embrace a daily form of death.

Death to hopes and dreams.

Death to finances.

Death to our vision of what we wanted "family" to look like.

Yet, like a winter snow that eventually retreats to reveal the sprouting seeds beneath her cold blanket, it was a death that eventually gave birth to new life. Through the pain and difficulty, we experienced something we never imagined—an unexplainable peace. The more we found ourselves chasing after the passions of Jesus, leaving behind those things in ourselves that so often interrupt his radical nature, we became more peaceful than ever before.

More at peace than when our finances were whole.

More at peace than when our family was whole.

More peace than had we never decided to live lives of radical love.

We discovered that following the radical message of Jesus meant that we were being invited into a life of undiluted difficulty—a life that apart from Jesus would make relatively no sense at all.

Following the American Jesus, on the other hand, is relatively easy. This Jesus can be followed by way of a short, simple prayer, attending church, and following a list of cut-and-dried rules, to which most people can eventually acclimate. Following the authentic Jesus, however, is much, much more difficult.

The real Jesus? Well, if you want to follow him, he's sure to complicate things and ask you to leave behind some hopes and dreams in order to pour yourself out in the service of others. The radical message Jesus taught is the way to eternal life, not through power and control, but through giving yourself up, and laying your life down. We find life by becoming willing to first experience forms of death.

Anyone who loves their life will lose it, while anyone who hates their life in this world will keep it for eternal life. Whoever serves me must follow me; and where I am, my servant also will be. My Father will honor the one who serves me (John 12:25-26).

It's a radical message—but one that often gets diluted in American culture. Here we're focused on prosperity, individual rights, achieving our hopes and dreams…

But that's not Jesus.

The undiluted Jesus is someone who invites us to actually follow him—to do the things that he did—and to be willing to set aside anything in our lives that gets in the way of that central calling.

It's a calling for us to simply look like Jesus.

To let the dead bury the dead.

To embrace an uncertain future.

To pick up a cross.

If we want to rediscover the radical message of Jesus, we must stop diluting it by focusing on power, peace of mind, and prosperity. Instead, we must embrace the truly radical message that invites us to find life through laying it down.

Ironically—if we do this—we'll actually find the life we're looking for, unfamiliar as it may be.

CHAPTER 8

Undiluted Justice

But you have neglected the more important
matters of the law... (MATTHEW 23:23).

This is all Dean Borgman's fault, I kept telling myself. Had my wife never seen the listing for his class that semester, I might have avoided this entire mess.

Sleepless nights? Could have been avoided.

A million ambulance rides? Could have been avoided.

Calling mobile crisis teams to help us de-escalate situations? Could have been avoided.

Spending every dime of my life savings to help prevent two girls from ending up in a life of exploitation? Could have been avoided.

It *all* could have been avoided, had I never met Dean. Certainly I would never have selected his class on my own—it was entitled Biblical Global Justice. I still remember Tracy calling to me from the next room, saying, "Babe, I really think you should take this Wednesday night class next semester. It fits into your schedule perfectly and it sounds really interesting." That conversation forever threw a wrench into what could have been a comfortable life spent chasing the American dream.

But as we've seen, the guarantee of being comfortable isn't part of the deal with Jesus.

Judging from the title, I wasn't sure if Biblical Global Justice was a class on God's wrath and anger toward the nations, or some hippie propaganda that Glen Beck had warned me about. While my previous understanding of God's justice had been consumed with connotations of anger and wrath, by this point I had begun to realize how very wrong I had been about so many other things, and wondered if "justice" might be more than anything I had previously understood.

Well, it was.

Before meeting Dean, I was sure that the problem with American Christianity was that we had lost sight of just how pissed off God really is. Instead of being honest about an angry God who is so fed up with our abortions and same-sex marriages that he frequently sends his justice upon us by way of natural disasters and terrorism, I was convinced that we had diluted our idea of God's justice to make him seem a little too loving and a little too merciful. Between campfire sermons on judgment and hell, and watching every episode of two seasons of Way of the Master, talk of God's "justice" came naturally to me.

Justice, in my old paradigm, was all about the many different ways an angry deity would gleefully seek his revenge for all the little rules we neglected to follow. For me, God's justice simply meant that he'd never skip out on a good opportunity to punish me for something; and that when I got to heaven, justice meant he was going to play every secret moment of my life on a big movie screen for everyone to watch. For others, God's justice meant that they too would not escape his just wrath that would one day punish us without mercy for every last sin we'd ever committed.

The other type of justice I was familiar with was the social type—something (I thought) that had nothing to do with God. This was the type of justice I had no desire to explore—I already knew it was a bunch of socialist nonsense that wanted to uplift the poor even though "poor people are only poor because of their own laziness and bad choices." I had heard that there were some liberal Christians out there who would twist a few verses to make it seem like we were responsible for caring for the poor, instead of the poor being responsible for picking themselves up by their bootstraps like good ole Americans. If this were a class designed to turn me into a communist, socialist, or anything other than a good Republican (like all Christians are), I wasn't interested.

But I went anyway and figured if I got bored I'd catch up on Sarah Palin's twitter feed.

I warmed up to Professor Borgman right away. He was a gray-haired Episcopal priest, warm in his demeanor, but also a straight shooter who was extremely passionate about the content he was teaching. While I had been mentally conditioned to see members of the Episcopal church as being liberal hybrids of Christians instead of the real deal, something about Dean's passion for justice—and the fact that he'd spent a lifetime putting his money where his mouth was, became something that was admirable and contagious. Week after week I found myself challenged by a new understanding of "biblical justice" in a way that was the final straw in prompting an entire paradigm shift. Until that point, some days I had one foot in my old world and one foot in my new world; but all that quickly changed— my house of cards finally collapsed, and I had never been more relieved.

Justice, as it turns out, isn't so much about God's anger as it is his love. I discovered justice not as God throwing a violent tantrum, but God's passion for restoration, liberation, healing, and wholeness. Justice was no longer something to be feared, but something I wanted to participate in with every fiber of my being. In order to arrive at this place however, required me to set aside an obsession with retribution in regards to the concept of justice, and forced me to enter the Kingdom like a little child— willing to rethink and relearn.

In doing so, I finally discovered that we dilute the message of Jesus— and the entire message of scripture—when we leave out the centrality of *biblical* social justice.

Week after week as we went deep into the theme of justice in the Bible, I realized more and more that my lack of appreciation and understanding of biblical justice was a major contributing factor to a diluted Christian faith. It had become a faith that was great news for me, and possibly good news for some others—but not a radical, countercultural way of living that was good news for *everyone*. As the truth about justice began to sink in, I knew life was about to change radically for me.

Many of us have a diluted understanding of the biblical concept of justice due in large part to the culture in which we find ourselves. Western culture is a guilt and innocence oriented culture, meaning that we view all of our ethical questions through a lens of what would cause one to be guilty or innocent, right or wrong. While we might assume that all cultures see things through this lens, we would be wrong—many other cultures view ethical questions through a "shame vs. honor" paradigm while some others view their culture through a "fear vs. power" lens. Because we find ourselves situated in a guilt vs. innocence culture—which is a limited view of experiencing the world around us, we also have a limited concept of justice. Justice, in our culture, is largely reduced to themes of "punitive justice," where justice becomes an action that punishes a wrongdoer; supposedly righting whatever wrong took place (which it never does). While this is in fact one aspect of justice, it is not the holistic understanding of biblical justice.

Justice, as we see it throughout scripture, is less focused on punishing wrongdoing and more concerned with restorative actions designed to bring peace, restoring wholeness to society. When we see themes of justice in the Bible, we quite often see "justice" repeatedly associated with particular groups of people whom God points out are especially in need of our care and protection: the poor, oppressed, vulnerable, widows, orphans, and immigrants. Justice, as we see it in scripture, is defending and caring for the most vulnerable of society so as to restore them to their rightful place, beside us.

Not exactly the less than encompassing version of "justice" I grew up with.

Throughout the Old Testament, God repeatedly points out these classes of people who are typically marginalized; He teaches Israel that if they want to follow his heart, they must do so by caring for the vulnerable in their society. As one reads through the Old Testament with an eye open to seeing God's concern for the poor and oppressed, it's as if we're reading a book we've never seen before. We're quick to memorize "an eye for an eye" but have conveniently left out God's radical command to "do justice."

In Deuteronomy chapter 15, we find God prompting Israel for what it will be like to live in the Promised Land. God tells them that as a nation they will have enough wealth and resources for everyone, and that as a result, "there should be no poor among you." He goes on to warn them about being "mean-spirited" or "tight-fisted" when they encounter poor people, and that they should lend to them freely—even if they think they will never be repaid. God goes on to incorporate safeguards into the law that governed Israel to ensure that justice for the poor and oppressed was something that didn't get overlooked and relegated to being a neglected aspect of the law. He goes so far as to instruct them that they were not allowed to harvest their garden more than once—that they were to specifically leave behind anything they overlooked as well as their second crop so that this food would be available for the poor, immigrants, orphans, and widows.

The concept of redistribution of wealth, as it turns out, was actually God's idea.

As we flip each page of the Hebrew Scriptures, we see that God's justice is overwhelmingly focused on the principle of the more affluent of society caring and protecting the weaker members of society. Those within the culture knew this quite well, and realized that close to God's heart was justice for the poor and vulnerable. In fact, in the story of Job we see Job himself cite the performance of social justice for the poor and needy as being central to his own defense before God:

> All who heard me praised me.
> All who saw me spoke well of me.
> For I assisted the poor in their need
> and the orphans who required help.
> I helped those without hope, and they blessed me.
> And I caused the widows' hearts to sing for joy.

Everything I did was honest.

Righteousness covered me like a robe,

and I wore justice like a turban.

I served as eyes for the blind

and feet for the lame.

I was a father to the poor

and assisted strangers who needed help.

I broke the jaws of godless oppressors

and plucked their victims from their teeth

(Job 29:11-17 NLT).

Why would Job specifically cite justice for the poor, orphans, widows, disabled, and immigrants as central to his defense? I think it's because he realized what we see expressed in the Old Testament prophets, in that living a life pursuing justice for the vulnerable isn't considered optional to God. At times in contemporary Christian culture, justice for the poor can be seen as a nice thing to do, but miss the fact that living a life that cares and advocates for the vulnerable of society is actually something God sees as being a *requirement* of following him.

As we see in the prophet Micah:

With what shall I come before the Lord and bow down before the exalted God? Shall I come before him with burnt offerings, with calves a year old? Will the Lord be pleased with thousands of rams, with ten thousand rivers of oil? Shall I offer my firstborn for my transgression, the fruit of my body for the sin of my soul? He has showed you, O man, what is good. **And what does the Lord require of you***? To act* **justly** *and to love mercy and to walk humbly with your God* (Micah 6:6-8)

We also see a similar command given by the prophet Isaiah:

Learn to do good.

Seek justice.

Help the oppressed.

Defend the cause of orphans.

Fight for the rights of widows

(Isaiah 1:17 NLT).

God's original design for culture was that caring for the poor and vulnerable would always be in the forefront of the minds of those with power and influence. Unfortunately, the nation of Israel often lost sight of this ideal and drifted into seasons in their history where their culture looked a lot like ours does today. They were a highly religious people, yet the rich were getting richer and the poor were getting poorer, with the most vulnerable of society being systematically neglected, instead of purposely cared for. Through the prophet Amos, God reveals that social justice for the poor is so central to what it means to follow him, that he's not interested in our religious activity if such religious activity is absent social justice:

> *I hate all your show and pretense—the hypocrisy of your religious festivals and solemn assemblies. I will not accept your burnt offerings and grain offerings. I won't even notice all your choice peace offerings. Away with your noisy hymns of praise! I will not listen to the music of your harps. Instead, I want to see a mighty flood of justice, an endless river of righteous living* (Amos 5:21-24 NLT).

Ouch.

God hates our religious activity when it is absent social justice for the vulnerable. Yet in our culture we've diluted the concept of justice for the poor, the immigrant, and the disabled into something that's "nice to do" instead of something that is central to our identity as God-followers. Even worse, in many respects, as Christianity has been married off to right-wing politics, it's even safe to say that social justice is despised in much of contemporary Christian culture. Immigrants, the poor, and the sick have all too often been viewed as what's "killing our country" instead of the precise objects God has called us to love and care for with reckless abandon.

We've missed the centrality of social justice in the message of God and traded it for a diluted version that tastes nothing like the original.

We are not alone in diluting this aspect of the message of God. The religious elite of Jesus' day had completely missed the point as well. By the time we see Jesus begin his ministry, we find the culture of first century Israel to be yet again separated by a rich vs. poor divide. While this was in part due to the Roman occupation that levied astronomical taxes, the poor were also being driven deeper into poverty by the practices of tax collectors and religious leaders. The powerful—both Roman and Jew—were getting richer, and everyone else was relegated to the margins of society.

Once again, the poor had been forgotten.

In the lead-up to Jesus beginning his earthly ministry, God attempts to remind the nation of Israel about the centrality of social justice as if he's warming them up to rediscover the radical message in a new way. Most of us have probably heard our fair share of sermons on "repentance," and it's true that as John the Baptist prepared the way for the nation of Israel to meet their Messiah, he went around the countryside baptizing people and preaching that they needed to "repent." Eventually people started to ask John what it meant to repent, and how they should repent. What I find most interesting about John's response when folks asked him, "How should we repent?" was that there were 613 laws in the Old Testament, which would have given him a long, long list of potential broken rules they needed to repent of. However, John doesn't talk about smoking, drinking, premarital sex, rock music, or any of the other things we hear mentioned in Americanized sermons on repentance—instead, he tells them that if they want to repent, they need to start engaging in social justice for the poor:

> *The crowds asked, "What should we do?" John replied, "If you have two shirts, give one to the poor. If you have food, share it with those who are hungry"* (Luke 3:10-11 NLT).

Biblical repentance, as taught as a gateway introduction to the message of Jesus, was an invitation to be generous toward the vulnerable, honest in our dealings, and content with what we have.

Not exactly the version of repentance we often hear. As John finishes paving the way for Messiah, we see Jesus roll into town preaching the same message of justice—good news, for the poor.

From the first moments of his ministry, Jesus reminds us of God's concern for the poor and vulnerable, and reminds us of the centrality of social justice. In his first sermon, Jesus publically declares that he has come to "preach good news to the poor"; and when he confronts the religious rulers in Matthew 23, he tells them that even with all of their religious activity, they've missed the "more important" aspect of the law—justice and mercy, reiterating for them the command given through Micah. Finally, in his most provocative statement on social justice, Jesus actually teaches that highly religious people who are not engaged in social justice for the poor and vulnerable, *don't make it into heaven.* Jesus said:

> "But when the Son of Man comes in his glory, and all the angels with him, then he will sit upon his glorious throne. All the nations will be gathered in his presence, and he will separate the people as a shepherd separates the sheep from the goats. He will place the sheep at his right hand and the goats at his left.

> "Then the King will say to those on his right, 'Come, you who are blessed by my Father, inherit the Kingdom prepared for you from the creation of the world. For I was hungry, and you fed me. I was thirsty, and you gave me a drink. I was a stranger, and you invited me into your home. I was naked, and you gave me clothing. I was sick, and you cared for me. I was in prison, and you visited me.'

> "Then these righteous ones will reply, 'Lord, when did we ever see you hungry and feed you? Or thirsty and give you something to drink? Or a stranger and show you hospitality?

Or naked and give you clothing? When did we ever see you sick or in prison and visit you?'

"And the King will say, 'I tell you the truth, when you did it to one of the least of these my brothers and sisters, you were doing it to me!'

"Then the King will turn to those on the left and say, 'Away with you, you cursed ones, into the eternal fire prepared for the devil and his demons. For I was hungry, and you didn't feed me. I was thirsty, and you didn't give me a drink. I was a stranger, and you didn't invite me into your home. I was naked, and you didn't give me clothing. I was sick and in prison, and you didn't visit me.'

"Then they will reply, 'Lord, when did we ever see you hungry or thirsty or a stranger or naked or sick or in prison, and not help you?'

"And he will answer, 'I tell you the truth, when you refused to help the least of these my brothers and sisters, you were refusing to help me.'

"And they will go away into eternal punishment, but the righteous will go into eternal life" (Matthew 25:31-46 NLT).

Those who feed the hungry and give water to the thirsty make it in; but those who don't, get sent away into "eternal punishment"? That's hard core. Strange that I've never heard this mentioned during an altar call—ever.

Tough stuff to wrestle with, but this is the radical message of Jesus—and caring for the poor and vulnerable is central to it, whether that makes us comfortable, or not. So central, in fact, that Jesus himself said that if you're not caring for the vulnerable, you don't make the final cut.

While it's not the doing that gets us in, the doing is what shows we have a heart that has been reconciled to God's way of doing things.

If we want to rediscover an authentic Christian faith, we need to start being honest with ourselves in that our attitudes regarding social justice and caring for the poor have often been more influenced by our own political culture rather than being influenced by the radical message of Jesus. Whereas our culture often reduces the Christian faith into something that is characterized by right believing (orthodoxy), Jesus indicates that right believing goes hand in hand with right doing (orthopraxy). And the orthopraxy he speaks of is a little different from the version we're often given: he's not talking about refraining from drinking and smoking, and avoiding premarital sex—he's talking about living radically generous lives that go out of their way to care for and protect the vulnerable of our world.

One of the barriers to living a life of undiluted justice becomes our own cultural concepts of what justice is and what it looks like. Far too many of us have been led to believe that social justice is the same thing as socialism, that it's linked with liberal politics, or that it's somehow outside the realm of Jesus. Justice, in the biblical sense, is none of those things. Simply put, living a life of justice is to live a life where we seek every opportunity to fix what is broken, to heal what has been wounded, and to make the world a little more right.

People who do undiluted justice are simply the people who are trying to make the world a little less broken.

A little more reconciled.

A little more whole.

A little more beautiful.

People who do undiluted justice are people who realize that God isn't interested in our hollow religious activity. Instead, he wants to see by how we love others, that he really and truly has our hearts.

He wants to know that we love him—but the love language he wants us to use as we express that, is doing justice toward others.

Often we sponsor a child for $39 a month and write letters four times a year and call it good. But I think Jesus is looking for something a little more radical—a little more counter to our culture.

Jesus, I think, wants more.

I think he wants us to see radical giving to those in poverty—not as charity, but as justice. I think he wants to see us use our voices to speak up for the oppressed, not as something to check off our list but as a matter of justice. I think he wants us to set aside our own selfish ambitions so we can more freely give of ourselves to others—because it is just and right to do so.

Embracing a life that is characterized by undiluted justice is one more aspect of following the radical Jesus that will be a ticket not to prosperity, but to sacrifice. However, as with the other aspects of following the radical message of Jesus, this too becomes a form of death that births a radical new life. It may *appear* to be death, but it's not.

It's birth.

To many outsiders looking in, my life during this chapter certainly appeared to be falling apart. What they were really witnessing, however, was a radical rebirth. The death they witnessed was simply the death of my old self; the death of someone who wanted to live for himself but chose to die instead. The rebirth they witnessed was the birth of a man who realized a life best lived is a life given freely for someone else.

The invitation to do undiluted justice was just one more invitation to embrace the radical message of Jesus that invites us to inherit life by first embracing our death.

When we die to ourselves, we also die to want. In turn, dying to want gives birth to generosity. Generosity, as one will discover, is a rebirth into a satisfying life.

Yes, all the therapy, ambulance rides, and sleepless nights were hard—but setting aside my selfish ambition in order to offer family to children who otherwise would never have a mom and a dad? That's been life-giving, even when I count the horribly high cost I have paid.

Undiluted justice may look different in your life—all of us are called to live and express it in different ways. Yet I remain convinced that you too will discover new life as you embrace the radical message of Jesus, which invites us to radically set ourselves aside in order to more freely serve others.

Embracing this death and becoming willing to discover new life is the first step in a life of undiluted justice.

Had my life never seen that class listing, all of this could have been avoided.

So, yes—I guess you can say that my life now is all Dean Borgman's fault.

For which I am deeply thankful.

CHAPTER 9

Undiluted Love

But I tell you, love your enemies... (MATTHEW 5:44).

As I continued to embrace living in the tension of following Jesus, learned what it meant to live in undiluted community, and began to give so much of my life for the pursuit of justice—the pursuit of making the world a little less broken—I came to more fully appreciate that this new life wasn't a mental decision, but a radical reorientation of my entire being, and the adoption of a lifestyle that probably wouldn't make sense to a lot of people—including other Christians. Yet as I experienced the life-giving aspects of actually living out my faith in a more authentic way than ever before, I knew there was no turning back. In fact, at this point in my journey I knew it was likely that I would continue to find more areas of the faith that had been diluted by the cultural waters I had spent so many years swimming in.

As I began to process the tremendous pain Tracy and I experienced from our adoption story, I realized that I had unintentionally stumbled upon another diluted area of Christian faith in our culture—one that if exchanged for the radical message of Jesus would be life-giving spiritually, and life-giving culturally. For more than a year, we had lived in a home that was plagued with violence. Not more than a day or two would go by without some sort of violent episode that put all of us in danger—we had both been physically assaulted multiple times, I had almost been stabbed on more than one occasion, we had obnoxiously loud alarms installed on our bedroom door to wake us in the night if the door was opened, and on countless occasions had to call in friends from our undiluted community to come and take our youngest daughter, Johanna, while we waited for the police to arrive and disarm our oldest. We were all too well acquainted with violence.

As I looked back at the very real, violent, and even life-threatening situations I had faced, I realized that I had never once considered responding to my daughter with violence in kind. This however, isn't anything profound—I can't imagine how anyone could use violence against their own child, even when their own life was in danger. However, I could have responded violently many, many times, and I would have been legally justified in doing so, as there were countless occasions when dangerous weapons were involved, and real lives—especially mine—were at risk.

There is no way, however that I would violently harm my own family, even to protect my own life. Due to the fact the violence I experienced was at the hands of a family member whom I deeply love, I instinctively was more willing to allow my own life to be taken than I was willing to take another's. That's what it looks like when you have undiluted love: you're willing to lay down your own life, and you become unwilling to take someone else's life—even when they intend to harm you.

Love, in the purest form, places a higher value on the life of someone else than what we place upon our own life. While responding to violence with nonviolence out of love for the offender might make perfect sense in a familial relationship, we wouldn't often apply this concept to relationships outside of that immediate family or closer personal friends. When it comes to people we love, responding to violence with nonviolent love is almost instinctive—yet if experiencing violence at the hands of a stranger or enemy, responding to violence with violence is often considered the "right" or acceptable thing to do.

Contemporary culture—including Christian culture—sends us a very different message on the use of violence than what we find in the radical teachings of Jesus. We live in a country where the Second Amendment to the U.S. Constitution is propped up to idol status, a culture that is obsessed with our right to use violence when we feel it is justified, and a country where some estimates indicate that there might actually be more guns in the land, than people who inhabit it. Oftentimes our political candidates who most publicly align themselves with the Christian population of the country are also the candidates who most strongly support unrestricted gun rights. In fact, it is hard to imagine that a Christian political candidate who supported gun restrictions would have any real chance at having widespread support by the Evangelical Christian community. In our culture, we love our weapons and we don't want even the slightest curtailment in the right to have, carry, and use them.

We're not satisfied with weapons designed for hunting; we want the right to have military-grade weapons.

We're not satisfied with handguns that only shoot six rounds at a time; we want guns that can kill in mass quantity.

We're not satisfied with the right to have weapons at our home; we want the right to hide them under our clothing and carry them wherever we want.

We haven't had our lust for violence satisfied by the fact that children are so often the innocent victims of gun violence—instead, we argue that the best solution to gun violence is for more people to have more guns. In typical American fashion, we are never satisfied—even when it comes to violence, death, and destruction. We now find our culture caught in a never-ending cycle of violence, and somehow along the way the followers of Jesus have become complicit in that cycle.

The lust for violence, our rights, and the idolatry of self-perseveration has infiltrated Christian culture to such a degree, and for so long, that this aspect as much as any other, has diluted our faith into something that looks nothing like Jesus. Yet, once again as fish who can't recognize the water they are swimming in, many of us spend years walking through life with the unchallenged assumption that our American Christian attitudes toward violence somehow fit within a paradigm of following Jesus.

Unfortunately, they don't. Jesus doesn't look like a gun-toting American, and a gun-toting American doesn't look anything like Jesus. If we want to rediscover a more authentic faith—a faith that is actually counter to culture instead of completely in line with culture—if we want to rediscover a faith that embraces God's "higher ways" more than it does faulty human reasoning, we must rediscover the radical teachings of Jesus regarding undiluted love and nonviolence.

Understanding the teachings of Jesus and the cultural context within which he taught, reveal to us that Jesus not only understood what it was like to live in a violent society, but that the culture of Jesus' time faced far more violence than you or I could imagine. The Jewish people had endured years of violence and oppression throughout their history, sometimes being taken away into captivity and other times by occupation in their own land—oppression and violence was deeply ingrained into their cultural memories. During the time that Jesus lived and ministered, the Jews were under violent and oppressive Roman occupation where the Romans controlled most aspects of their lives. While the Jews were allowed to maintain many of their traditions and even had their own, limited court system, they were expected to live compliantly with the "enemy." Any deviation from compliance with the occupation led to violent consequences—most notably, the practice of crucifixion that was so ghastly and done in public that it served as a rather effective warning that insurrection would not be tolerated.

If anyone had the right and good reasons to use violence against enemies, certainly the Jews of Jesus' time would be counted among them. Various Jewish groups had different views on how to best navigate living under a violent occupation. Some preferred to segregate themselves from society and went out to live in the desert. Others, such as religious leaders and tax collectors, cooperated with the oppressors in order to enjoy wealth and power. Still others, this group called the Zealots, favored a more obvious approach: violent resistance. The Zealots (such as the disciple, Simon the Zealot) came to believe that a violent overthrow of the Roman occupation would be the only way they would ever again experience freedom—and they had convincing reasons for believing violence was the answer. Of all the hot issues of Jesus' time, the issue of how to respond to Rome—violent oppressors—was probably at the top of the list.

There were a lot of ethical questions tangled up in the question of responding to Roman occupation. During the ministry of Jesus, he responds to the various viewpoints in this regard—sometimes subtly, and sometimes directly. However, of all the opinions people held, Jesus seems to speak out most strongly, and most often, against the use of violence. Even given the ripest conditions possible to make a convincing case for the use of justified violence against an oppressor—far more compelling factors than what we face in our culture—Jesus instead teaches that those who actually "follow" him, will opt out of the never-ending cycle of retributive violence, and instead opt to respond to violence with radical, undiluted love.

What Jesus teaches in regard to violence is so radical that it almost doesn't even make sense. When we serve an Americanized version of Jesus, we tend to subconsciously imagine that Jesus would have said something to the effect of, "Don't use violence unless you really and truly fear that your life may be in danger." However, that isn't what he taught—Jesus repeatedly taught that those who actually "follow" him must adopt a position of non-violent love of enemies. This new ethic of nonviolence was not what people were expecting; the Mosaic Law had established principles that justified retributive violence (much like in our own culture), condoning tit-for-tat responses to injustices. Jesus insists, however, that the Kingdom he came to establish was going to operate by different principles from anything they had experienced previously, and that the use of previously justified violence had no place in this new movement God was starting.

In Jesus' most famous sermon of his public ministry, the Sermon on the Mount, Jesus outlines the new cultural principles that are central to the new "Kingdom" God was starting through him. Throughout the sermon he hits on a wide range of topics, all of which bear importance to this new culture Jesus envisioned. Central in this sermon however, Jesus radically overturns the law and establishes a new Kingdom principle of nonviolence:

"You have heard that it was said, 'Eye for eye, and tooth for tooth.' But I tell you, do not resist an evil person. If anyone slaps you on the right cheek, turn to them the other cheek also. And if anyone wants to sue you and take your shirt, hand over your coat as well. If anyone forces you to go one mile, go with them two miles. Give to the one who asks you, and do not turn away from the one who wants to borrow from you.

"You have heard that it was said, 'Love your neighbor and hate your enemy.' But I tell you, love your enemies and pray for those who persecute you, that you may be children of your Father in heaven. He causes his sun to rise on the evil and the good, and sends rain on the righteous and the unrighteous. If you love those who love you, what reward will you get? Are not even the tax collectors doing that? And if you greet only your own people, what are you doing more than others? Do not even pagans do that? Be perfect, therefore, as your heavenly Father is perfect" (Matthew 5:38-48).

My favorite lines in all of scripture start with "You have heard that it was said…" because every time Jesus says these words, what comes out of his mouth next typically reverses the cultural paradigms people are used to. In the Sermon on the Mount, we find the same thing. For generations the culture had accepted retributive violence as something that was justified under certain circumstances. But what does Jesus say? Jesus tells them, "Hey, look, I know this is the way it has always been, and I know this is the way that seems best to you—but God is starting something new, and if you want to be part of this something new, we're going to do things differently from here on out."

The message of Jesus is not what they were expecting—it didn't fit nicely into any of the prevailing paradigms of the day. Neither does it fit into the paradigm we find so common in American Christianity subculture, which still operates on the same system that Jesus came to overturn. When Jesus says that they weren't to "resist" evildoers, everyone would have known who he was talking about—the Roman oppressors who consistently used violence toward them. When he argues that they should not resist, he's arguing that they should not fight back using the same tool (violence). While responding to oppressive violence with our own seemingly justified violence may make sense to us, Jesus teaches us that there's no place for that in this new movement that God is building.

Not only does Jesus teach that we are to nonviolently respond to our enemies, he goes on to teach us something far more radical. Responding with nonviolence isn't enough—he actually wants us to actively love our enemies with undeserved generosity.

After Jesus finishes overturning Jewish law that permitted retributive violence, he goes on to teach that we're actually supposed to be willing to "go the extra mile" out of love for our enemies.

"If your enemy takes your shirt, generously give up your coat also."

"If your enemy asks you to walk a mile, generously walk a second mile."

They expected a warrior Messiah who would free them from Roman oppression, but all they got was an itinerant preacher who told them to love and serve their enemies.

What a letdown.

Refraining from responding to violence and oppression with our own violence and oppression but instead choosing to respond to these things with an undiluted love is at the heart of the upside-down, countercultural message of Jesus. If we want to participate in this something new that God is doing, opting out of these violent systems that so easily influence us is not enough—he also wants us to also opt in to a system of radical, unspeakable, unexplainable love of enemies. In fact, Jesus includes in this teaching something that ought to invite us back into undiluted tension: he actually claims that loving our enemies is the path to being called "children of our Father in heaven."

Which means, if we're packing heat so that we can shoot someone who is stealing our television, we are *not* children of our father in heaven.

And if we're not children of our father in heaven—by my count—that leaves only one other option.

In the last moments of Jesus' life, we see that he wasn't just a crazy teacher who spouted off countercultural sayings—he was someone who lived perfectly what he taught others to do. In the Garden of Gethsemane we find perhaps the one instance in all of human history where the use of violence would have been best justified—protecting the Son of God from an unjust, violent death. However, when Peter takes out his sword and wields it in self-defense, cutting off the ear of the high priest's servant, we don't see an American Jesus applauding with approval. Instead, we see Jesus do two things: First, he rebukes Peter for using violence, telling him that whoever "lives by the sword will die by the sword." Second, we see that Jesus responds to his enemies not with violence, but with love and generosity, as he heals the man's ear.

Jesus' rebuke to Peter serves as both wisdom and warning. "He who lives by the sword will die by the sword" is a reminder to Peter that violence is an angry animal that is never completely satisfied regardless how well fed you keep it. In fact, the more you feed it, the more this beast craves more. The nature of retributive violence is that each instance of violence, no matter how well justified, simply invites more violence in return. We see this principle play out in small and large scales all the time. For example, after terrorists attacked the United States on September 11, 2001, the nation responded with what it felt was justified violence in the form of warfare.

However, whatever positive results some may argue resulted from the wars, it is an inescapable fact that these wars have, to some degree, created more terrorists. They hit us, so we hit them. In turn, they grow angrier and more determined to hit us back in retaliation, which would in turn result in us hitting them even more. Retributive violence is never satisfied, no matter how well justified it may seem at the time.

The early followers of Jesus understood this well and adopted lifestyles that embraced nonviolent love of enemies—opting instead for the role of peacemakers. The early church not only embraced the nonviolent teachings of Jesus, but also those of Paul who reiterated Jesus' teaching on nonviolence—even taking them one step further, twice declaring that anyone who has not agreed to a life of nonviolence was not fit to serve as a Christian leader. Although they too lived in violent cultures and could have expressed a well-sounding justification to use violence against their enemies, they instead cultivated a culture that demonstrated an undiluted love of enemies. They courageously opted to starve this insatiable animal instead of feeding it, and often paid for that decision with their own lives. This early Christian culture that embraced undiluted love lasted nearly 400 years into church history—until Christianity became the dominant religion of the Roman Empire, permanently infusing a willingness to use violence into Christianity, which has lasted even until today.

This isn't how it always was, and it's not the type of culture Jesus intended us to cultivate. When we look back at Jesus standing before Pontius Pilate, we find Jesus revealing that nonviolence was at the heart of the new Kingdom God was building. In fact, Jesus argues that the commitment to nonviolent love of enemies is proof that his Kingdom is actually from God:

> *"Are you the king of the Jews?" he asked him.*
>
> *Jesus replied, "Is this your own question, or did others tell you about me?"*
>
> *"Am I a Jew?" Pilate retorted. "Your own people and their leading priests brought you to me for trial. Why? What have you done?"*
>
> *Jesus answered, "My Kingdom is not an earthly kingdom. If it were, my followers would fight to keep me from being handed over to the Jewish leaders. But my Kingdom is not of this world"* (John 18:33-36 NLT).

Telling words, Jesus reveals.

"My Kingdom is not an earthly kingdom. If it were, my followers would fight…"

Participating in the Kingdom God is building through Jesus means that we are unwilling to use violence against our enemies. Being unwilling to use violence against our enemies, and instead choosing to express undiluted love toward them—regardless of cost to ourselves—is what leads to us being "children of our Father in heaven" as Jesus taught in Matthew.

Once again we find Jesus inviting us to embrace death, in order to actually experience birth.

Death…to our right to retaliate.

Death…to our own false sense of control.

Death…to the never-ending cycle of retributive violence.

Birth…to trusting God.

Birth…to a new way of living.

Birth…to seeing others the way God sees them.

Birth…to radically embracing undiluted love of others—especially our enemies.

When we let go of our own need and desire for power and control instead opting to embrace the radical principles of living in God's Kingdom, we find a peace we never knew was possible. During the many times when I would have been legally and morally justified to use violence to protect myself against a violent family member, I opted to refuse to see her as a violent threat to be eliminated. Instead I viewed her as my child, and God's child. Recognizing the divine image inside her made it impossible for me to ever consider harming her—regardless of cost to myself. I was willing to die for her, but was unwilling to harm her.

Strangely enough, I was at total peace.

Most parents, I imagine, would respond as I did. When you love someone, causing them physical bodily harm is simply unimaginable. Yet I've come to realize that treating only those we love this way—becoming willing to die by their hands before we killed them with ours—isn't enough, and isn't being fully true to the radical message of Jesus. To be faithful to the radical message of Jesus, we must extend that same love to everyone we encounter.

Jesus reminds us again, "In that way, you will be acting as true children of your Father in heaven. …If you love only those who love you, what reward is there for that?" (Matthew 5:45-46 NLT).

Agh. The hard stuff.

If I only love my own *child* nonviolently with an undiluted love…what makes me different from anyone else?

If you only extend a nonviolent, undiluted love toward those whom you love…how does that show you've opted to live in a Kingdom that plays by a different set of rules?

Jesus reminds us that even the most despicable people we can imagine treat those they love better than their enemies—and he warns us to not act like them. Instead, Jesus calls us to something far more radical and to a way of living that almost makes no sense all—loving our enemies and neighbors in the same way we love our very own families. Jesus calls us to love the person breaking into our house or carjacking our vehicle the same exact way we would love our own spouse or children. This sounds insane, I know, but the radical message of Jesus is so countercultural, so against our instinct as human beings, that it often feels absolutely crazy. That's part of the reason why I love it so much; the message of Jesus is almost too insane to not be true.

Finally Jesus reminds those of us who would desire to follow him, that in order to do so we must "deny ourselves and pick up a cross." Jesus set aside everything and willingly picked up the cross, choosing to nonviolently love and die for his enemies instead of calling down 10,000 angels to smite them.

If we want to follow Jesus, he says that we must do the same thing. However, before we can pick up a cross and begin walking in the path of Jesus, we must first deny ourselves—setting aside our own personal right to retribution, setting aside the pro-violent messages fed to us by American Christian culture, and must let go of whatever is in our hands—especially weapons—so that we can grasp the cross firmly.

It's time to let go.

Let go of violent American culture.

Let go of our guns and weapons.

Let go of our insistence that we are in control of our future.

Let go of our "right" to harm others when we feel it is justified.

It's time to let all of this go...and return to the radical message of Jesus, which invites us to trade all these things for a lifestyle that offers undiluted love, to everyone.

CHAPTER 10

Undiluted Forgiveness

*But whoever has been forgiven little
loves little* (LUKE 7:47).

After graduating from Gordon-Conwell I took some time off to give my full attention to my family in hopes that we'd begin to experience a season of healing in all of our lives. After four or five months, I sensed a calling to return to Gordon-Conwell for a second Master's degree, this time in World Missions, and so I returned for the extra year to continue in Missiological studies. During that time I began to further awaken to an exciting life calling to continue serving the poor and vulnerable in various ways outside the borders of my own family, and even my own country.

Although I was excited about returning to seminary, this became an emotionally difficult chapter to push through. For the first time in a while, I had time to sit, relax, and contemplate—not just the future—but the past as well. Part of that process meant coming to terms with all of the hurts and disappointments I had experienced in the previous chapter—a process that wasn't easy for me. As I began to be honest with myself about the depths of my pain, heartache, and even anger, I realized that so many of my present hurts were tapping into past hurts.

At the beginning of the semester I went through the usual routine of buying books to cover all of the required reading for the upcoming year.

Regardless of the class, the professors sure did value heaping a ton of reading on us, and each trip to the bookstore usually resulted in me juggling and dropping an armful of books as I attempted to safely tuck into my grasp all of the required titles. Books, in seminary, have a way of piling up on you—both in the bookstore and throughout the semester. Perhaps the best advice I ever received was from my preaching professor who told us it would be a good idea to keep track of all the required reading so that we could do it after graduation. I've certainly tried.

Keeping up on all the required reading that year wasn't always easy. As much as I wanted to dive deep into each text, emotionally I wasn't able to be present much of the time and those books kept piling higher and higher. One night as I had another restless night's sleep with my mind recalling all the hurt and disappointment I had experienced in life, I looked over at that growing stack of books and realized they were far too like my growing stack of hurt and disappointment—they just kept piling up and encroaching on my ability to fully embrace day-to-day living.

Deep hurts don't go away quickly.

Like my stack of books, if we don't proactively stay on top of hurts— properly managing the disposition of each one—we eventually roll over one sleepless night to see a growing stack of baggage that isn't going anywhere unless we take control and do something about it. The more we look at it, the more the thought of dealing with it suffocates us. The longer we put it off, the larger that stack gets—until we realize that at any moment, the world around us could topple over.

Perhaps the most difficult thing about hurts is they have a way of bringing up other hurts that have long been buried inside. Like a partially healed wound that we mostly forgot about, new hurts come along and bump up beside old hurts, tearing the wound open all over again. Before we know it, we're not just feeling the pain from our most recent hurt, but begin feeling pain from some really old hurts that we completely forgot about or didn't even realize were there. Like a domino effect, there are seasons in life when we feel like we're experiencing one hurt after another to such a degree that we can barely think, function, or make it through the day.

New hurts remind us of old hurts.

Fresh wounds tear open partially healed wounds.

Current disappointment triggers prior disappointment.

Oftentimes our present situations would be emotionally manageable if it weren't for all that damn baggage that gets pulled out of our closets with every new injury. Being wounded in life—for whatever reason—is a vicious cycle because of the way new hurt always tends to trigger old hurt. Some days we don't know if that force keeping us in bed with the lights out is something from our present or past—all we know is that hurt becomes so overwhelming, it dominates us.

As I began to come to terms with this dominating force of compound hurt, I began to realize that while there is an element of hurt we can't control, there is an element to dealing with hurt that we *can* control. In regard to the latter, I came to accept that I had been unwittingly playing right into its hand all along. My present condition, hurting over not just the present but also the past, was something I had contributed to, both passively and actively.

Of all the things I've been good at in life (which is actually only a couple of things), one of my finer skills has been keeping track of who or what has hurt me in the past. Whether they intended to or not, neatly tucked away in my mind was an intricate list of every person and every instance where I had ever been hurt or wounded. These were more than simple memories of being hurt—memories and wounds aren't our fault and can't be controlled. Rather, instead of passing memories that were out of my control, I realized that I had held on to my past emotional baggage by way of failing to forgive those people or situations that had previously wounded me.

I had a book of childhood hurts, marital hurts, career hurts, parenting hurts…

I had a big stack of hurts, and they were suffocating me.

The equally difficult yet freeing realization was that the stack of books that began to encroach on my life—the ones chronicling all the hurt I had experienced—had actually been written by me. Not only did I write them; I was holding on to each one for safekeeping. To give myself a false sense of control over situations where I didn't always have control, I chronicled my unforgiven hurts and piled them on top of each other until they got so high that the stack was at risk of toppling over.

I realized that if I wanted to experience life as it could be, something needed to change—the old way of living wasn't working for me anymore. Like a crazy cat lady who doesn't throw out a newspaper for twenty years, eventually our hurts pile up so much around us that nothing else—good or bad—can fit in. I realized it was time to clean house, and start getting rid of the old junk that wasn't serving me anymore.

As I began to sort through my book of hurts, I slowly began to rediscover what is perhaps the most practical aspect of the radical message of Jesus, and one that would invite me into a lighter, freer, and more abundant life—undiluted forgiveness. In one of his parables, Jesus tells a strange story that's often called the "Unmerciful Servant." In this parable Jesus tells competing narratives of two servants who each had a stack of books like mine. When confronted by the reality of the book, each servant responds differently, and experiences a different result. The parable, as Jesus told it, goes like this:

> Then Peter came to Jesus and asked, "Lord, how many times shall I forgive my brother or sister who sins against me? Up to seven times?"
>
> Jesus answered, "I tell you, not seven times, but seventy-seven times.
>
> "Therefore, the kingdom of heaven is like a king who wanted to settle accounts with his servants. As he began the settlement, a man who owed him ten thousand bags of gold was brought to him. Since he was not able to pay, the master ordered that he and his wife and his children and all that he had be sold to repay the debt.

"At this the servant fell on his knees before him. 'Be patient with me,' he begged, 'and I will pay back everything.' The servant's master took pity on him, canceled the debt and let him go.

"But when that servant went out, he found one of his fellow servants who owed him a hundred silver coins. He grabbed him and began to choke him. 'Pay back what you owe me!' he demanded.

"His fellow servant fell to his knees and begged him, 'Be patient with me, and I will pay it back.'

"But he refused. Instead, he went off and had the man thrown into prison until he could pay the debt. When the other servants saw what had happened, they were outraged and went and told their master everything that had happened.

"Then the master called the servant in. 'You wicked servant,' he said, 'I canceled all that debt of yours because you begged me to. Shouldn't you have had mercy on your fellow servant just as I had on you?' In anger his master handed him over to the jailers to be tortured, until he should pay back all he owed.

"This is how my heavenly Father will treat each of you unless you forgive your brother or sister from your heart" (Matthew 18:21-35).

While referring to "debts," Jesus is actually telling a story about two different ways of dealing with a growing stack of hurts. The word debt is an easy substitute for some form of hurt requiring forgiveness; because when we are wounded, something is taken from us, setting us up in a debt-to-debtor relationship, whether we want to be or not.

And so, the story might better be called, "A Story of Forgiveness vs. Unforgiveness."

The main character in the story owes a massive debt—one that given multiple lifetimes, he would never earn enough to repay. Realizing his own inability to make the debt right, he asks and receives forgiveness from the one to whom he owed the debt. However, he immediately goes out and changes roles, this time becoming the one who is owed a debt—yet it is a very insignificant one. When the servant is placed in the position of extending undiluted forgiveness or grasping on to unforgiveness, he refused to forgive. Instead of mercy, he threw the man into prison.

The story tells two ways of dealing with hurts: forgive freely, or demand a repayment that can't be repaid, regardless how big or small the debt is.

You can't repay a hurt—there is no way to emotionally replace what has been lost. No matter how badly we want to erase our pain and disappointment, and no matter how badly we think the person who hurt us is actually able to replace the loss, you often cannot repay hurt.

It's usually impossible.

The king in Jesus' story demonstrates for us the only healthy way to deal with debts that can't be repaid. When he realizes that his servant has no way to repay what has been lost, he's faced with a choice—let the stack of books get taller, or grant forgiveness so that he can be free from the oppressiveness of keeping a record of debts. In his wisdom, he realizes that no matter what he chooses, he's never going to get back what had been taken from him. Continuing to keep an accounting of everything he had lost was only going to harm himself.

No one had to live with that stack of books, other than the king. Just like when you and I keep an ever-growing pile of hurts, no one has to deal with the inner turmoil other than our own selves. The king realized that the only way to live free from the oppressive force of hurt and loss, was to forgive—and get rid of the stack of books completely.

The servant who had just received unmerited forgiveness is quickly faced with the same choice as the king, but chooses a different path. When immediately confronted with an opportunity to extend forgiveness—in the story it is over a much lesser amount than what he was forgiven—he refuses. Like the king in the story, he had been keeping a record of his loss, but unlike the king in the story he decides to live with his books instead of extending forgiveness.

It is a choice that doesn't work out so well for him. Jesus tells us that the king called the servant back, and had him thrown into prison to be tortured.

Because he chose unforgiveness, the servant finds himself in a prison of his own choosing.

The servant had the opportunity to live in freedom, but he chose to live in miserable isolation and torture. In this story, both the king and the servant had a record of debts—a record of things taken from them and a list of people who took them. Both wanted to get back what they had lost, but those who had taken from them were unable to make the situation right. This placed both characters in the same predicament: live in misery with the stack of books looming over them, or forgive the debt. Both made opposite choices, and Jesus reveals to us the natural outcome of those choices.

You and I have something in common with both the king and the servant—we are all pretty good at keeping a record of hurts and the names of those who have hurt us. Also like the story, the most common case we find ourselves in is that the ones who have caused our hurts, who have taken something from us, are either unwilling or unable to make the situation right. As a result, those books on our nightstand tend to get stacked higher and higher. And so, you and I face the same choice as the king and his servant. Do we forgive so that we can clear that stack of books off our nightstand? Or do we hold on to them and allow ourselves to be tortured by the contents inside?

The way of Jesus is the way of forgiveness, the way of freedom—but our way is a straight-and-narrow path that leads straight to a prison bench with a stack of books looming over the nightstand.

Once we start to open up this parable told by Jesus, we discover the truth that forgiveness is actually an act of mercy toward ourselves, instead of an act of mercy toward the one who has hurt us. So often in culture, we see forgiveness as letting someone who has wronged us off the hook; when really, forgiveness is something that lets *us* off the hook. Forgiveness says that we are unwilling to be tortured even one second longer.

The radical message of Jesus tells us that we've been misunderstanding the nature of forgiveness all along—forgiveness isn't what sets them free, it's what sets us free.

You and I both have a stack of books, and if we're honest with ourselves, I think we'll realize that doing things our own way only makes that stack of books get higher and higher. Given enough time, we find ourselves in an emotional prison with just our own selves and the books. The radical message of Jesus, however, reminds us that this is a prison that is locked from the inside and we alone have the power to unlock the door and walk out into wide open spaces in complete freedom.

Without the books.

CHAPTER 11

Undiluted Loyalty

No one can serve two masters (MATTHEW 6:24).

Rediscovering the radical message of Jesus became not an isolated event but instead became a new way of living. As I continued to wrestle with the changes I was experiencing, I came to realize that Jesus wasn't simply inviting me to change my viewpoint on a few isolated issues, but was actually inviting me into a lifelong process of continually discovering new, countercultural ways of living. While I wanted to embrace these countercultural principles with my entire being, in many ways I also felt like the Stretch Armstrong toy I had as a kid—no matter how hard I pulled his arm, there was an unseen force that would snap it back in the opposite direction. Such was the same with embracing the radical teachings of Jesus. When embracing this new way of living pulled me one way, I could often feel the not-so-subtle pull of culture (quite often, Christian culture) trying to yank me in the opposite direction.

Embracing community was life-giving, but I still felt culture telling me that I should be able to do this on my own. Learning to live in the tension was more freeing than living in constant certainty, yet culture seemed to nag in my ear that I should have less doubts about this Jesus stuff. I began to discover that inclusively loving the outsider felt right in my head, but I also had to deal with this worry that perhaps I was becoming a little too "liberal" since living like Jesus caused me to move in a right-to-left trajectory. Nonviolently loving my enemies seemed to make absolute perfect sense, yet conservative Christian culture kept gnawing in the back of my mind, telling me that keeping that gun loaded and in my nightstand would actually be the "loving" thing to do.

Relearning to follow Jesus was a lot more work than it was the first time around, because there was a lot of unlearning that needed to take place first. While I worked to finish my second Master's from Gordon-Conwell, I continued to find myself in a constant process of attempting to deconstruct values that were cultural and replace them with the legitimate teachings of Jesus—no matter how crazy that made me look to the world or Christians around me. On one hand this process of parsing out the true origin of my beliefs and replacing when appropriate was reinvigorating; on the other hand, it was also exhausting. The constant, never-ending, Jesus vs. all the cultural influences around us, push-and-pull cycle is exhausting work—culture is ingrained deep within us, and it takes a potent combination of time and self-awareness to figure out what is culture, and what is actually Jesus.

As hard as it is, it must be done if we want to rediscover the radical message of Jesus in a way that actually renews and revolutionizes our lives.

The hell-fire preachers of my past would often shout from the pulpit, "Jesus wants all of you," as they encouraged people to come forward and invite people to pledge their loyalty to Jesus by "asking him into their hearts" (even though such a term isn't found in the Bible). As I look back on my experiences with those types of preachers, I realize that on many issues, they were completely wrong. Wrong on what following Jesus looked like, wrong that following Jesus was a simple business transaction, and wrong on a whole lot of things.

However, they weren't wrong on the issue that Jesus wants all of us. The way of Jesus is something that demands undiluted loyalty—because anything else makes following Jesus ridiculously impractical, and will quickly lead to feeling like that Stretch Armstrong I had as a kid—pushed and pulled in a million directions without any clear sense of direction. The way of Jesus is supposed to be life-giving, but it's not when our arms are constantly being pulled out of their sockets.

Getting a concept half right can be just as destructive as getting it completely wrong—sometimes even more so—because in the latter case we let go of any self-awareness and are lulled into the false idea that we've somehow arrived. Far too many of us are taught an understanding of being loyal to the way of Jesus that is only half right; we're taught that one must follow Jesus—and only Jesus—yet we are simultaneously invited to embrace both American culture and Christian subculture in America. These cultural forces become so dominate to our new world that we quickly lose sight of where Jesus ends and where external culture begins. A message that at first sounded radical and counter to culture becomes something that fits right into the new paradigm we are directly and indirectly encouraged to adopt.

This wouldn't be a problem if American culture looked like Jesus or if American Christian culture looked like Jesus—but quite often, neither does. Jesus is a figure who presents a new way of living that is so radical and counter to our instinct that it doesn't fit into any cultural construct. Jesus wanted to change both secular and religious culture; he didn't want to simply fit neatly into it. Yet this is what we've done—we've slowly developed a concept of Jesus that fits neatly into our own cultural experience, allowing us to believe that we can somehow be equally loyal to our culture and Jesus at the same time.

We can't.

Since Jesus is in a category completely his own, it's simply not feasible to actually follow him while following something or someone else at the same time. Jesus himself taught on this general principle, teaching his followers:

> No one can serve two masters. Either you will hate the one and love the other, or you will be devoted to the one and despise the other (Matthew 6:24).

What Jesus teaches is that no two ways of living are identical. As a result, it's simply impossible to give equal loyalty to more than one way.

Unless both "masters"—both ways of living—are exact clones of each other, we will eventually end up being pulled in conflicting directions, which will either force us to make a choice or remain in the middle with our arms pulled out of their sockets. Dividing loyalty between the way of Jesus and anything else—even if it looks "Christian"—won't work in any practical sense. If we actually want to follow in the footsteps of Jesus, we have no other option than to set aside any other loyalty that could ultimately give us conflicting direction.

Giving the way of Jesus our undiluted loyalty doesn't mean that we're able to eliminate all of the competing forces that vie for our loyalty. We are people living in a certain time and in a certain place, and unless we are able to completely separate ourselves from the entire time/space continuum, we're going to experience competing forces that beg for our attention. Throughout the Bible God seems to understand this as well; and instead of giving us the impossible task of eliminating everything that might possibly seduce us, he instead encourages us to simply put our priority and loyalties in the right place.

Perhaps the best example that God understands the constant forces that have the potential to detract from our primary loyalty to him is found in the first commandment God gave to Moses. When God first spoke the Ten Commandments to Moses, the first commandment he read reveals that he understands our predicament of dividing our loyalty between his way, and the ways of our own culture. The commandment reads: "You shall have no other gods *before* me." The nuance of the language in this verse hints that God understands all of the competing cultural forces around us and realizes that, try as we might, it's impossible to completely rid ourselves from all of the many things that seduce our affection and loyalty. What he does ask us to do, however, is give to him our primary loyalty—not to put any other gods *before* him. The moment we realize that something else is becoming the object of our devotion and loyalty, God wants us to set that—whatever that is—aside, and offer him our devotion. It is impossible for two objects, two people, two philosophies, two ways of living, two anything, to share primary loyalty.

There's only room for one.

As Jesus reminds us, no two masters have the same goal—a truth that has the potential to create utter frustration in any potential follower. During my years in the United States Air Force (prior to becoming an Anabaptist, obviously), one of the most frustrating scenarios was when we received conflicting orders from two different leaders. Military culture expects unwavering obedience and execution of any lawful order you are given, but is run by human beings who don't always share the same opinion or goals. While most of the time having multiple leaders worked just fine, there were plenty of times when we received different directives from different leaders—prompting the question, "Who's order do we follow?" Receiving conflicting orders from conflicting people makes it impossible to follow both—there can be loyalty to only one. When we attempt to please both of them, Jesus tells us that we're on the fast track to hating one and loving the other—a position that doesn't bode well if we're seeking to live lives of peace and meaning.

Divided loyalty doesn't work on any practical level. As Jesus reminds us, it actually will make us completely miserable. Jesus wants us to experience a life that's far more "abundant" than anything we could think up on our own; and to do that, Jesus invites us to reorient our lives so as to give his teachings our undiluted loyalty.

The challenge we face is that for too long we've been trying to serve more than one master without even knowing it. Instead of seeing ourselves primarily as followers of Jesus, we've grown to see ourselves as Americans, Calvinists, Charismatics, Anglicans, Conservatives, and a million other identities that subtly compete with Jesus for our loyalty. While these labels aren't necessarily bad or destructive, they become bad and destructive when placed out of order—receiving our primarily loyalty and becoming our primary identity, instead of allowing Jesus himself to fill that position. Given enough time and enough circumstances, all of these nationalistic, tribal allegiances will ultimately clash with the countercultural teachings of Jesus, and will force us to choose between Jesus and other loyalties, even if we don't always realize it is even happening.

This lack of self-awareness in our divided loyalty has resulted in a Christian culture in our country that, ironically, doesn't always look like the Christ it claims to follow. We're loyal to the principles of our country, citing the second amendment as if the apostle Paul penned it. We're fiercely loyal to John Calvin as if he was the 14th disciple and responsible for writing the lost second half of the New Testament. We're loyal to our Protestant tradition, carrying forward hundreds of years of disdain and skepticism toward our Roman Catholic brothers and sisters, as if the Roman Catholic tradition were a form of radical Hinduism. We're loyal to identity after identity…loyal to everyone except Jesus.

A person can't serve two masters, Jesus says.

It shouldn't be shocking when people are interested in Jesus, but don't want anything to do with American Christianity. To outsiders, it looks like we can't pull it together and even decide who or what we're emulating. To insiders who actually give Jesus a shot, they find a religion that's loyal to principles, theologies, and traditions, but are often completely unable to find the Jesus of scripture anywhere among us. As a result, people are miserable and the church in America is dying, while an entire section of the population is left searching and craving a different way.

While the church thinks these people are walking away from a life of following Jesus, they're actually walking away because they're hungry for a Jesus that's a little more applicable and a little more radical than what they're being served up by the American church.

They're walking away because they're looking for the undiluted Jesus, but far too often aren't finding him in churches that worship Jesus without actually following him.

When we begin pouring out some of the cultural waters that have diluted our concept of what it means to follow Jesus, we find that Jesus offers us something better, something timeless, and a way of living that is outside of any cultural label we want to put on it. For those of us tired of religious categories, tired of the left vs. right divide, and tired of a hollow religion that offers little peace and even less meaning, we find that Jesus offers us a third way—a way that's available to us regardless of the cultural waters we may find ourselves in.

This alternative way of living was something Jesus called "the Kingdom." From the first pages of the New Testament throughout the entire teachings of Jesus, we find that teaching people how to live in the Kingdom was a central theme. When John the Baptist announced that the Messiah was about to be revealed, he went around telling people that the "Kingdom of God" was about to arrive and to prepare to start living differently. Jesus continued this message as he was first introduced to the public, telling people to stop living according to their cultural standards (repent), and adopt a radical new lifestyle as part of the "the Kingdom of God." In a world being progressively pulled between secular culture and religious conservatism, Jesus offered a radical third way—he invited people to enter into and start living in his Kingdom. This Kingdom living was something that secular culture wasn't interested in, and something that offended religious conservatism—but to those thirsty for a radical new way of living that brought peace and meaning to life, it became something that was too good to walk away from.

The third option of Kingdom living is a doorway to radical new life. In fact, Jesus actually called living in the Kingdom "life eternal." Those who have decided to embrace undiluted loyalty and live lives according to a Kingdom culture that doesn't fit into any earthly paradigm know exactly what Jesus was talking about—it *is* life eternal. Part of the beauty of Kingdom living is the dichotomy of the Kingdom; it is something that exists in the here and now but is also something that has not yet been fully realized. As Jesus describes eternal life in the Kingdom, he is both describing the way things will be in eternity but also describing a new way of living right now. The invitation to enter the Kingdom and embrace living in accordance with these timeless cultural values is an invitation to start living our lives right now, as if we're already in heaven. When we accept the invitation and give this new cultural framework our undiluted loyalty, something within our spirit cries out, "Yes! This is how we were meant to live!"

But entering "The Kingdom" is hard because these new cultural values often contradict what we've been taught and pull against all the other cultural forces around us.

In the culture of The Kingdom, it isn't the rich and the powerful who are blessed—it's the poor.

In the culture of The Kingdom, it isn't the self-reliant who find life, but those who realize their reliance on others.

In the culture of this new Kingdom, it isn't the powerful who find blessing—but the meek who reject the need to have power over other people.

In the culture of this new Kingdom, the ones who are blessed are the ones who mourn—realizing they are different from the culture they find themselves in, and are constantly reminded they are immigrants living outside their home culture.

In the culture of this new Kingdom, the ones who find true life are the ones who develop hearts for justice and mercy, seeking to make things a little less broken in anticipation for the ultimate reconciliation in the age to come.

In the new culture, the blessed ones are the people who are open to the ways of God, rejecting alternative cultural frameworks in favor of Kingdom living.

This new cultural framework—this Kingdom—is so radical, so upsidedown and backward to anything else we've ever experienced, that it can be challenging to embrace it. Those content to live in a culture devoid of God reject it as outright foolishness. Those who have embraced a Christian religion that is married to American culture find it equally bizarre and will find ways to explain it away in order to assuage their own conscience, allowing them to think they're following Jesus while also retaining anti-Kingdom values such as the pursuit of power, hoarding wealth, and the use of violence. The people who sign on to this new way of living are often the people we'd least expect. During the ministry of Jesus, he warned the religious conservatives, telling them, "The tax collectors and prostitutes are entering The Kingdom ahead of you!"

Are there people entering ahead of us?

What we have failed to fully realize is that it is entirely possible to be a "Christian" but not enter this new way of living that Jesus calls "The Kingdom." This is precisely what was happening during the time of Jesus—the religious were content with their religious culture, and when invited into a radical new way of living, they opted to reject life in the Kingdom in favor of rigorous religion. Entering The Kingdom means that first we have to leave an old one, however good and comfortable that previous kingdom may seem.

This means that those of us who are restless, marginalized, powerless, or outcasts actually have a special advantage when presented with the option to join The Kingdom, because it's easier for us to forsake an old allegiance and embrace a new one. The fewer old things we're carrying in our arms, the easier it is to reach out and embrace this something new that Jesus is doing in the world.

This new Kingdom Jesus describes begs us to embrace it.

If we are content to keep living however we're living, life in The Kingdom is less than appealing. But for those longing for something more, who realize their own brokenness, and are willing to switch loyalties to a new culture? These few who are searching for deeper purpose and value, something new, something radical, and something with eternal significance—these people find that life in The Kingdom is the satisfaction of their deepest longings.

Life in Kingdom culture is more backward than anything we've ever experienced, but is a taste of heaven on earth.

Life in Kingdom culture means letting go of so many things that are hard to let go of, but as we do, we find a peace and new life.

The radical message of Jesus is that we need not be absorbed into whatever cultural framework we find ourselves in. Instead, we are invited to begin living as immigrants who reside in a foreign land but who retain the value system of our home culture as we live out our lives. The downside is that we will be in a constant state of mourning as we experience daily reminders that we're outsiders. Yet, as we embrace our home culture, we find meaning and identity that simply doesn't exist in this strange place we live.

And so, Jesus invites us to choose where we want to place our undiluted loyalty—culture or Kingdom?

Do we place our undiluted loyalty in our country, our tradition, our religion, or do we funnel our loyalty into new life in "The Kingdom"?

We can only choose one—because no one can serve two masters. The beauty of this choice is that when we declare ourselves "all in" for this new thing that Jesus is doing, we find ourselves—as I went on to discover—wrapped up in a story that is bigger than we ever dreamed.

CHAPTER 12

Undiluted Story

*All this is from God, who reconciled us to
himself through Christ and gave us the ministry
of reconciliation* (2 CORINTHIANS 5:18).

There's nothing more frustrating than watching a movie after you've missed the opening scene. When we haven't understood how the story started and where the story is headed, we miss the joy of submersing ourselves in the story because we're spending so much of our mental energy trying to figure out the plot and the role of each character within the story. For me, this is especially frustrating if I'm watching the movie with my wife (who doesn't like movies). We laugh and joke about this now, because every experience is the same: I spend half of the movie fielding questions about what is happening and why. My response to her is always the same, "I have no idea...I'm watching the same movie you are." Eventually we're able to catch on to where the story has been, where the story is headed, and finally grow to appreciate the role of each of the characters participating in the unfolding of the story.

You and I have found ourselves in the middle of a story that has been unfolding since the birth of time. From the first pages of scripture up until the very end, we see that God is writing a story and that everyone who has ever lived has been invited to play a role in the story. Whether we want to or not, we are all characters on God's divine stage—appearing for just a brief scene that is part of a much, much larger unfolding. In order to experience our lives as God has intended, we need to rediscover this undiluted story and uncover our very specific roles for the current act that is being played out in the here and now.

All good stories bookend an introduction and conclusion that play off one another; a compelling introduction points to the conclusion of a story, and the conclusion of a story reminds us of what happened in the opening scene. The story God is writing is no different—the introduction points to the conclusion, and the conclusion brings us right back to the beginning when it all began. In the book of Genesis, we see that God created humanity to live in unbroken relationship with him, in a created world where God resided with humanity. Scripture tells us that God actually walked with Adam and Even in the coolness of the day, giving us visual imagery of humanity living in and caring for a perfectly created world where God was directly present. However, like any compelling story, something in the original plan went way, way wrong, and set us on a course that was different from what was originally intended.

When we look at the conclusion of God's story as told in scripture, we see that the conclusion is almost identical to the introduction. Once again, the world will be made right, creation will be restored, the nations will be healed, and once again God will reside in a perfectly created world in unbroken relationship with humanity.

God returns.

God restores.

Finally, heaven comes to earth for good.

In the final chapter, God's will being done on earth as it is in heaven, as Jesus prayed, will finally become a permanent reality.

You and I have found ourselves sandwiched between an introduction we didn't experience, and a conclusion that has yet to be realized. Just like jumping into a movie partway, you and I could experience a lot of frustration in discovering our part in the story if we don't first step back and take a 50,000-foot view of what has happened, and what will happen.

As individuals, we crave purpose and meaning in our lives. Books on discovering purpose fly off the shelves, and people of all faiths seek to discover meaning in this present existence. While there are a lot of competing narratives for discovering purpose and meaning in this current life, I strongly believe that the only way we will ever be able to experience purpose and meaning to the fullest, is when we understand and finally embrace our individual role in the undiluted story in which we have found ourselves.

In the 1800s Gustav Freytag argued that all compelling stories follow a similar five-part structure. He defined these elements of a story as: Exposition (the introduction), Rising Action (building toward a climactic moment), Climax (the turning point of a story), Falling Action (the part of the story where the results of the climax are experienced), and finally, Resolution (the stage where everything returns to the calm experienced in the beginning).

The undiluted story we find ourselves in, God's story, seems to follow this same pattern. In the Exposition stage of the story we see humanity living in a perfect creation and in unbroken relationship with God until the plan goes awry with the introduction of sin. In the Rising Action stage, we see God systematically setting the stage for the arrival of the Messiah—Jesus—who would build a new Kingdom that would have "no end." In the climactic chapter of God's story, we see God incarnate in the person of Jesus, who came to inaugurate the Kingdom and to destroy the works of the devil. The story will ultimately end with a stage of Resolution, where everything returns to as it was in the beginning—creation is restored, sin and death are eliminated, and God resides in unbroken relationship with humanity, forever.

Caught between the climax that was the life, death, and resurrection of Jesus and the ultimate resolution of this story, is the stage of Falling Action.

Which is where you and I find our own undiluted story.

In God's divine plan, you and I were born into the stage of the story where the effects of the life, death, and resurrection are played out, as the story moves to an ultimate, beautiful end where everything is reconciled and permanently restored. We are caught up in the now but not yet, the inaugurated but not fully realized, movement toward ultimate resolution of everything God created and pronounced "good." We are the people caught between the two most exciting parts of the story, and we have a role to play if we embrace our part in this divine unfolding. For many of us, we've missed the grand beauty of this stage and our own roles within it. Instead of consistently keeping our eye on the complete story, culture has slowly diluted and obscured our ability to understand the big picture of this drama by way of reduction and hyper-focus on only isolated elements of the story. However, when we rediscover the radical message of Jesus, we find that this story is bigger and more beautiful than we ever realized—and so is our individual role in how this plays out.

When I first arrived at Gordon-Conwell, one of the first items on the new-student checklist was to meet with our assigned advisor. Apparently there was a shortage of advisors in the Theology department, so I was assigned an advisor from the Christian Counseling division. She was a wonderful person who became a family friend, but wasn't able to advise me in my theological studies. I realized that if I valued the role of an advisor in my own story, I would need to seek out an unofficial advisor/mentor on my own.

During my first semester, I met Dr. Vidu, a new theology professor from Romania. Through his class, Emergent/Emerging Theology, I was able to finally find freedom in my theological exploration and subsequently establish some meaningful friendships with the folks I mentioned in the Undiluted Community chapter. After that first class, I quietly decided that I was going to take every class Dr. Vidu offered, whether I needed it for graduation or not, and that I was going to make him my unofficial advisor without even asking.

When I first signed up to take Recent Theories of the Atonement with Dr. Vidu, I had no idea how dramatically the class would reshape my understanding of my role in God's story. Prior to that experience, my complete understanding of the climactic moment of God's story, (the atonement gained through Jesus), had been diluted by a truncated, legal understanding of what was accomplished on the cross. Stemming largely from theologians during the reformation who had backgrounds as attorneys (as well as medieval understandings of reclaiming one's honor), many cultures have slowly seen the big picture of the atonement reduced to a simple, individualistic legal transaction.

The diluted version of the story goes something like this:

You and I are horrible, totally depraved sinners.

Our sin has earned us the wage of death that will be paid to us by burning in eternal conscious torment in hell. Forever.

Jesus came, lived a sinless life, absorbed the wrath of God, and was punished in our place on the cross.

Because Jesus paid our fine, you and I can be legally set free and experience eternity in heaven if we repent and place our faith in Jesus.

This, is the diluted gospel.

It's not that this way of understanding the gospel is totally incorrect—it's not. It's just totally reduced and simmered down into something that is infinitely less than what the big picture actually reveals. Understanding the nature of the atonement via this diluted version of the gospel has some unintended consequences. Mainly, this understanding of the gospel causes us to see our place in this story as simply being people who invite other people to accept Jesus so they can be legally adjudicated "not guilty" and go to heaven.

Which is great. I'm all about people following Jesus and going to heaven.

It's just that the story is so much bigger than that.

The radical message of Jesus is that you and I are part of a bigger story, and have a bigger role to play than what we have probably realized. If we want to rediscover our place in the story, we need to step back far enough until we can once again see how big this story actually is—and rediscover the beautiful role we are invited to play.

For nearly the first 1,000 years of Christianity, followers of Jesus had a bigger understanding of the story—something that is often called

"Christus Victor" in Latin. Under this understanding of the cross, Jesus was seen as the victor over the works of the devil (see 1 John 3:8), and that he was accomplishing a reconciliation of "all things" to himself (Colossians 1:20). This "classical" understanding of what Jesus accomplished kept the picture big, very big.

However, because of theology born out of guilt vs. innocence cultural frameworks, time has diluted the work of Jesus into something that simply reconciles individual humans to God. While it is true that Jesus reconciles humans to God, this isn't the whole story and is an incomplete way of helping us find our role in this story. The undiluted version, however, is that Jesus is the victor over the works of the devil, and that he has begun a process of reconciling everything.

Everything.

He's reconciling humanity to himself.

He's reconciling humanity with each other.

He's reconciling creation.

Jesus is reconciling everything.

This is a reconciliation that has been inaugurated, but not yet fully experienced—but it will be, in the final chapter of the story. Until then, the story we find ourselves in is one where God is moving everything back toward the way things were in the beginning.

He is restoring.

Renewing.

Reconciling.

Everything.

Our undiluted role in this story is that you and I are invited to partner with God in the reconciliation of all things, as we move the world closer to the beautiful, final chapter. We each have a role in carrying this story forward.

Apostle Paul describes our role in God's story as a "ministry of reconciliation." We have all been given an invitation to partner with God in reconciling everything he made.

This is a big, big invitation—an invitation that gives us infinite ways to partner with God.

First and foremost, God certainly wants to reconcile *us*. We are not able to participate in our role in the story if we are not first reconciled to the divine author, and resurrected into something—someone—new. When we reorientate our lives on Jesus himself, embrace his radical new way of doing life, and begin walking in his footsteps, we experience resurrection in our own lives. We finally begin to taste the effects of the reconciliation Jesus achieved in his own resurrection.

Once we have experienced reconciliation and resurrection(s) in our own lives, we're invited to partner with God in helping others experience this too.

When we embrace our place in the story, we embrace the fact that God wants to reconcile and resurrect us, and he wants us to partner with him to accomplish new life in the story of others. In this world there is no shortage of broken hearts, broken dreams, and lonely drifters. Our role is to be a people who exist to bless others, who remove barriers people have to encountering God, and to be people who pronounce not condemnation—but reconciliation.

In many ways, we already knew that—but when we look at the bigger picture of God's story, we see that there is so much more to participate in. Too often our culture gets so caught up in the first element God is reconciling that we forget the others. There were many times as a teen when I heard preachers send the message that "Christian service" meant being a pastor or missionary for men, and the wife of a pastor or missionary for women. This sent the message that the only thing God is reconciling in the world is people to himself, and that if you want to partner with God, that's where the action is. However, that's simply not true—the undiluted story is bigger, and so is our place in that story.

Not only does he want to reconcile individuals to himself, he also wants to reconcile individuals to each other. Jesus references this in Matthew chapter 5 when he outlines what living in the Kingdom looks like—he says that it looks like a life of peacemaking. Peacemakers exist not simply to stop two sides from fighting, but to promote wholeness and reconciliation in relationships. Our place in the story means that we are invited to embrace peacemaking and reconciliation among nations, among races, in workplaces, in churches, in marriages, and in families.

Whenever we help people reconcile a marriage, whenever we help parents reconcile with their children, whenever we help anyone anywhere reconcile with another, we are embracing our undiluted role in the story. The Bible ends with an event called the "healing of the nations," and that's something we can begin working toward right now—starting with the reconciliation of small relationships and working up from there. Being a people devoted to peacemaking and reconciliation between people and people groups helps us demonstrate to the world the direction this story is moving in—it's moving toward a day when everything will be reconciled and all will be at peace, as it was in the beginning.

Finally, God is also in the process of reconciling creation, and we are invited to partner in that reconciliation also. In Western, hyper-individualized culture, we tend to think that everything is all about us—and we miss the forest for the trees, literally. Prior to creating humanity and saying "it is good," God first created the rest of creation and said "it is good." In addition to humanity, creation itself has felt the impact of what went wrong in the garden, and also has a place in God's story of reconciliation. As Paul writes in Romans 8:19-21:

> *For the creation waits in eager expectation for the children of God to be revealed. For the creation was subjected to frustration, not by its own choice, but by the will of the one who subjected it, in hope that the creation itself will be liberated from its bondage to decay and brought into the freedom and glory of the children of God.*

God's story begins and ends with creation in a perfect state of peace and harmony. Like us, creation has not experienced the fullness of that reconciliation yet—but we are invited to participate in it right now. If this story is moving toward bringing the environment into "freedom and glory," and if this story is moving back toward the beginning where God's original plan for humankind was to care for the environment on his behalf, we must embrace our role in that undiluted story right now.

Environmentalism, as it turns out, isn't just for hippies anymore. Finding our place in this story means that we are free to embrace the fact that God isn't just fixing us, he is fixing creation too, and invites us to partner with him. Partnering with God no longer needs be understood exclusively in terms of inviting people to be reconciled to God, but must also include peacemaking among others, and peacemaking with the environment. When we restore relationships between people, we find meaning and identity as we embrace a forgotten role in the story. When we care for and protect the environment, we are embracing God's original role for humanity and we are participating in a beautiful, divine story that ends not simply with a restoration of our souls, but a restoration of everything else that he made, too.

From the beginning of time, God has been writing a story. It began in a beautiful garden where he walked in the coolness of the day with us, and the story ends that way as well. However, we're not at the end of the story yet—God is still writing it, and we were all born as characters with a divine role. The story as it is in our time, is one of now but not yet, inaugurated but not fully realized, where God has given us the invitation to embrace our place in the story as "ministers of reconciliation."

But too often we settle for a diluted version of what is a big and beautiful story.

You and I were born to be people who reconcile things. Somewhere along the way this big picture of God's story became obscured as cultural influences diluted and then simmered down a big story into a little story. The radical message of Jesus, however, is that everything is in a process of reconciliation, and everyone is invited to participate.

You have found yourself in a story that you didn't write, but nonetheless, you have a part.

You were created to play a unique role in how this story plays out.

You were created to be one who helps to reconcile...

Everything.

CHAPTER 13

Undiluted Identity

The old life is gone; a new life has begun!
(2 Corinthians 5:17 NLT)

Some people say that going to seminary can cause one to lose his or her faith, and as I left Gordon-Conwell for the final time and moved on to doctoral work in Missiology at Fuller Seminary, I looked back over what had been a crazy journey of radical transformation and realized that had been a partially correct observation. The handful of years spent in Boston's North Shore had been a process of loss and growth, death and rebirth, and unlearning coupled with rediscovery. While I no longer recognized the man in the mirror, it was not due to a loss of faith, but a rediscovery of a more undiluted Jesus—a rediscovery that had left me with a new identity.

Prior to rediscovering the radical message of Jesus, my identity had been diluted with a host of other cultural factors—all of which detracted from experiencing a richness of new faith. During my previous decade in the military, my identity had been consumed with being "Sergeant Corey," and I derived all of my meaning in life from that identity. Once I left the military and returned home to quaint New England, my meaning and identity became wrapped up in being a good "Conservative" and a good "Republican," something that had become a core understanding of self and drove my identity. Still other times my identity was wrapped up in being

149

a "Christian," where cultural norms of American Christianity became the filter through which I understood my purpose and myself.

All that, I had learned, distracted me from discovering Jesus along with the identity that comes from a lifestyle of following him. I thought back to the meeting I had with my friend Joel during my crisis of faith and subsequent reorientation on the person and teachings of Jesus Christ. During that meeting, as Joel was praying for me, he said that God was in the process of giving me a "new name." While I didn't know what that meant back then, I do now. Making the serious life choice to live out the teachings of Jesus, regardless what label that earned me, was going to lead me into an entirely new identity that was so different from anything that existed before.

My new identity had simply become that of a Jesus follower.

We live in a world that is constantly fighting to control our inner narrative—a world that wants to dictate our identity. We are submerged in national culture, family cultures, work cultures, ethnic cultures—cultures of many sorts, all of which in one way or another try to dictate our identity. With every word from our parents, to every commercial we see on television, we are bombarded with messages about who we are, and who we are not. This bombardment of messages on identity results in our concept of self being pieced together by competing (often conflicting) narratives—all of which subtly beg our inner loyalty. Yet, the radical message of Jesus hasn't changed in over 2,000 years. It was, and always will be, the simple invitation of "follow me." When we accept that invitation, we are invited to leave all the other narratives behind, and to embrace a new identity as people who are simply trying to be like Jesus.

Jesus, I believe, wants us to find our identity in following him—without diluting that down with anything else.

Scripture tells us that when we decide to follow Jesus, we actually become a "new creation," and that is something I have found to be all too true. Nearly everything about my faith had changed in some way over the previous three and a half years, and the faith I ended up with was nothing like what I had expected this "new creation" to look like. Growing up, the idea of "if anyone be in Christ they are a new creation" meant something totally different from the way I see it today. In past generations, becoming this "new creation" simply meant that we ask Jesus into our hearts and then begin the difficult journey of conforming to American Christian culture—something that, instead of Jesus, becomes our new identity.

I am convinced that this isn't what Jesus had in mind. Jesus invites us into a radical, undiluted identity that won't fit within any cultural framework—not even Christian culture. The way of Jesus is a culture that is all on its own. Deriving our identity from any cultural influence that trumps Jesus, dilutes our faith into something that conforms with culture instead of something designed to be counter to culture.

Embracing this new identity in Christ isn't always easy. It might sound new, refreshing, and even exciting (and as we near the end of the book, I hope you're seeing it that way!), but adopting a new identity comes with adopting new lifestyle patterns—which is the hard part. This part of the faith is something that has always been accentuated, albeit poorly. Many of us are probably well acquainted with sermons that talk about the "change" that's supposed to happen in our lifestyle once we start to follow Jesus, and in principle, those preachers are right. However, when we start following the undiluted Jesus who is counter to culture, we find that this change in lifestyle is different from what we have so often been taught.

Under the old paradigm, following Jesus meant that I *don't* do all the things on the list I'd been handed. However, as I began discovering an undiluted faith I realized that following Jesus is more of a list of things you do, rather than things you don't do.

The invitation of Jesus is an invitation to embrace a new identity—one that looks radically different from any identity you've ever been offered or experienced before. For many of us, simply being a Christian by American cultural standards is no longer satisfying or fulfilling—we want an identity that's more. Jesus, I discovered, has been offering us this identity all along, but we've often missed it with the many ways we intentionally and unintentionally dilute the faith that is named after him.

Embracing an undiluted identity means that we are passionately dedicated to following the way of Jesus, regardless what that looks like. When

I first began to realize that I was becoming a different person by actually following Jesus instead of simply being a "Christian," one of the first things I said to my wife was, "Please don't tell anyone back home." I knew that following Jesus would mean that I'd become a man without a tribe—uneasy everywhere and at home nowhere. Yet, as I put one foot in front of the other and began following the radical message of Jesus, I found it to be so life-changing that I no longer cared what my old Christian community would think of me. I had found the Jesus who was more amazing and relevant than any version of the American Jesus I had ever met—and there was no turning back.

There still isn't.

In time, I was shocked that skeptics, agnostics, and weary Christians looking for something more became so interested in this undiluted Jesus I began telling them about, while so many of the religious elite no longer wanted anything to do with me. I received anonymous hate mail from somewhere among the church community that originally sent me off to seminary, had a long-time friend end his friendship with me, and numerous other encounters with the conservative Christian community that reminded me I was without a tribe. However, I also discovered that if the religious elite condemns us, but social outcasts want to come over for dinner to talk about God, we've arrived at something far more in line with the undiluted version of Jesus—because that was his daily reality too.

Embracing a new identity as a follower of the radical message of Jesus frees us. We find that we are no longer tied down to tradition, dogma, or cultural expectations, and that we are simply free to start doing the things that Jesus would do, and loving the people Jesus would love—without panicking about what other people may or may not think about it. We are free to embrace a new identity, to live life in a radical new way, and to leave behind anything that might get in the way.

The author of Hebrews described following Jesus as running a race. In chapter 12, verse 1, we are encouraged to shed anything that gets in the way of running this race of following Jesus. Too often we simply think of shedding the traditional "sinful" behaviors that we've been taught will get in the way of running this race—and that's great. We often fail to realize some of the more pressing obstacles in the path—often invisible obstacles placed in our way by our own cultural dilution of the message of Jesus. However, once we begin shedding those things that dilute the radical message of Jesus, we find that we are able to run the race set before us without such a heavy load on our backs. We become free to follow, free to be like him, and free to do the things he would be doing.

But we can't do that until we shed our old identity and adopt a new one.

When we focus on the "others" we think are diluting the message of Jesus but fail to first realize that we do it too, that becomes an obstacle to rediscovering a richer and more vibrant faith, because our focus is external instead of internal. However, when we realize that we also live out a faith that has been unduly influenced by our own culture, we're free to begin a process of deconstruction and rediscovery that leads to freedom and wholeness. We must realize that no one group or tradition has a monopoly on the undiluted Jesus, and that rediscovering him is a lifelong process of spiritual exploration. And so, we must have a "reset" moment in our faith where we humbly admit that our concept of Jesus might not be the full, complete, or most accurate version, and we do this by embracing a new identity as people recommitted to simply following the way of Jesus, whatever that looks like.

When we have our lives oriented on religious identity instead of on Jesus alone, we encounter a massive obstacle in our path. As was true with my story, orienting my life on a religious identity, religious tradition, or even a set of doctrines, got in the way of actually following Jesus. We must remember, as revealed in scripture, that it is entirely possible to be highly religious people, without following Jesus. However, Jesus invites us to set these identities aside and simply follow him. When we reorientate our lives on the person and teachings of Jesus, we become free to follow him wherever he leads—even if it is in an opposite direction as where our religious tradition might lead us. When we find our identity in anything other than Jesus, we're adding weight to our backs and slowing ourselves down. Instead, we must shed those things and clothe ourselves in a radical new identity by reorientating our lives on the person and work of Jesus, and nothing else.

As we adopt this radical new identity as Jesus followers, we must remember that this identity is not simply individualistic; it is communal. One of the first actions we see in the life of Jesus is that he surrounded himself with a core group of friends who were dedicated to living out this journey of faith, together. If we truly desire to follow in the footsteps of Jesus, we must do the same. We must remember that this life was not intended to be lived in isolation and with dependence upon rugged individualism, but instead was intended to be a life lived in unbroken community with others. When we put on this new identity as people who live like Jesus, we will find freedom and the abundant life Jesus promised in the authentic relationships we have with one another—always remembering that the hallmark of a believer is that we "love one another."

As we settle into our undiluted identity and actually begin walking in the footsteps of Jesus, we must always be attuned to the fact that Jesus was an outcast who came to love on other outcasts. The people who had been told they were out, are the people Jesus invites in. Whether sinners, tax collectors, prostitutes, or drunks, Jesus was the rabbi who invited the outcast to take a seat at the table. The main focus in his life was showing us how we can know and experience God, and he did that by constantly tearing down the obstacles that often prevented people from having a safe place to encounter the living God. As the people of Jesus, living lives patterned after Jesus, we too must develop a heart for the excluded, a passion for barrier breaking, and an unquenchable thirst for helping others find space (physically and emotionally) to experience the risen Christ.

Once we hit our stride in this quest of following Jesus, we're going to start to get to know him better. While this may sound great, we must also remember that Jesus was the guy who said a lot of things that made people uncomfortable. Jesus confronted empire with Kingdom, sin with grace, and violence with love, introducing to us a radical new way of living. For many of us, our culture has taken the edginess of Jesus and made it something designed to change others. However, we must remember that before the radical message of Jesus can change someone else, it must first change our own hearts. Once we turn our index finger inward and set down the tweezers we were using to remove the speck from our neighbor's eye, we are able to most fully experience a new identity that begins with the transformation of our own hearts.

As we slowly learn to grow comfortable with the radical message of Jesus, and as we learn to allow his words to radically transform us, we also grow more comfortable with the tension Jesus invites us into. Once we are able to accept life in the tension, we become free to adopt an identity that fully embraces him. When we pretend that we have all the answers and cling to our black and whiteness, we find that we are not clinging to Jesus himself but are instead clinging to our own assumed knowledge and confidence. The radical message of Jesus is that we can let go of our idolatry of certainty and instead embrace a new identity as people who are wrestling and growing, learning and unlearning, changing and morphing as we navigate the twists and turns of life. We're never going to have this completely figured out, and the beauty is that we were never meant to.

Looking back, the one thing that has taken me most by surprise in following Jesus is the level of undiluted difficulty. Sure, as kids we were warned about how hard it was to follow Jesus, but for all the wrong reasons. Following Jesus was going to be hard, so we were led to believe, because people of the world would hate us and want nothing to do with us. The reality I have discovered is that when we live lives that reflect Jesus, most people (with the exception of the religious elite, lovers of power, and lovers of money) actually love us—just like they did with Jesus! However, living a life that makes the gospel attractive is difficult—it means that we must get beyond ourselves, oppose cultural forces that dilute the beauty of the message, and embrace a life that is dedicated to doing undiluted justice. Committing our daily lives to being people who live to make the world a little less broken and a little more reconciled isn't easy—but it is beautiful. This new identity as people willing to do the messy work of reconciling people and reconciling creation is an invitation to lay our lives down and experience a death that will lead to a true rebirth.

Yet perhaps the most pressing barrier for many of us in following an undiluted Jesus is our tendency to hold on to past hurts and withhold forgiveness to those who have hurt us. When we maintain our stack of books and refuse to clean them off the shelf, we cling to elements of an old identity when a new, lighter identity awaits us. However, when we embrace a lifestyle of forgiveness and replace our old identity with one that offers a radical love toward ourselves, our neighbors, and even our enemies, we find that new life is free for the taking. As we forsake this old way of living— one that simply doesn't work—we are finally able to place our primary loyalty to a radical new lifestyle that actually does work and leads to the purest form of freedom.

The radical message of Jesus is that we are free to leave our old identities behind and adopt a new one.

When we finally give up control, lay down our own identity, and pick up our cross, we are finally able to discover our own place in this story.

Your role in this story is more beautiful and more different from anything you previously imagined.

After all these years, Jesus is still the guy who's offering us something different.

For those of us who are weary, burnt out, and ready to throw in the towel, Jesus offers us a different way of living that removes the burden, restores life, and leads to restoration and wholeness.

For those of us tired of stale religion that drains more from our tank than what is put back in, Jesus offers replenishment.

For those of us who no longer have the energy to orientate our faith on tradition and doctrine, Jesus offers us the opportunity to radically reorientate our lives on him.

For those of us who have spent years trying to hold it all together and who have exhausted ourselves by trying to do this on our own, Jesus offers us a radical new life where we all do this together.

For those of us who can't bear to continue on with an "us vs. them" mentality and who are tired of constantly judging who is in and who is out, Jesus offers us a new way of living that is no longer focused on declaring who is out, but instead is focused on embracing the outcast and inviting the outsiders to join us at the table—as equals.

For those of us who have grown discouraged because we thought the message of Jesus was supposed to be something simple and easy to understand, Jesus offers us a lifetime of learning and wrestling without ever having to pretend that we actually have it all figured out.

For those of us who have tried to do this, but realized we totally suck at it, Jesus affirms for us that it was never intended to be easy. Instead, Jesus invites us into a process of death and rebirth, falling down and getting back up, on a journey where he will be faithful to stick with us through every success, and every failure.

For those of us tired of belonging to a religion that seems to care about people's eternal suffering but overlooks the suffering happening right here and now, Jesus offers us a life dedicated to making the world a little less broken and a little more reconciled, right here, right now.

For those of us who are no longer comfortable participating in ancient systems of retributive violence that fail to solve real problems while only creating more violence, Jesus offers us the opportunity to opt out of the entire system. Instead, he invites us to respond to hatred and evil with love and mercy—freeing us from the burdens of retaliation and violence.

For those of us who have found ourselves locked in a prison of anger, bitterness, resentment, and unforgiveness, Jesus reminds us that this is a prison locked from the inside. He hands us a key and invites us to walk outside in free and open air, without the stack of books.

For those of us who realize we have been serving two masters and we've grown to actually hate both of them, Jesus offers us the opportunity to give him, and him alone, our loyalty, and to no longer care what label that earns us.

For those of us tired of feeling like we lack purpose or feel like our roles as Christians in the world is less than appealing, Jesus invites us to discover our place in the story—a big, beautiful story that has the role of reconciler waiting for us.

For those of us tired of the way Christianity and American culture have blended at the seams, Jesus offers us a radical way of living that transcends and runs counter to culture.

After all these years, Jesus is still offering us something different...

Something that is life-giving.

Something that results in freedom.

Something that is not burdensome.

Something that quenches our thirst.

Something that fills our hunger.

Something that opens our eyes.

Something that heals our wounds.

Something that gives meaning.

Something that restores our spirit.

Jesus offers us something that is...

Well,

Undiluted.

About Benjamin L. Corey

Ben is an author, writer, speaker, and minister.

He holds a Master of Arts in Theology from Gordon-Conwell Theological Seminary in South Hamilton, Massachusetts, a Master of Arts in World Missions (*Cum Laude*), also from Gordon-Conwell, and is a member of the Phi Alpha Chi Honors Society.

Ben is currently a doctoral student at Fuller Seminary for the degree of Doctor of Missiology. His field of study is church mobilization for the purposes of addressing cultural injustices; his dissertation topic is a discovery of the best practices of human trafficking aftercare which best promote shalom in the lives of those who have been freed from modern slavery.

He also serves as the Scholar in Residence for the Foundation for Hope and Grace and is a co-founder of the Not Here Justice in Action Network.

A lover of the miracle of adoption, he and his wife have chosen "adoption as a lifestyle," to show solidarity with the poor and vulnerable of this world.

He currently lives in Auburn, Maine with his wife Tracy and their Incan Cowgirl, Johanna (11).

Ben is a contributor for Sojourners, Red Letter Christians and Evangelicals for Social Action but can be primarily found writing at his personal blog, Formerly Fundie, on Patheos. To see what he's currently up to, just visit www.benjaminlcorey.com

Contact/Media Inquiries: contact@benjaminlcorey.com